MOUNT MARY
Milwaukee, Wi
WITHDRAWN

W9-ASG-956

Mother India's Children

OTHER BOOKS BY EDWARD RICE

The Prophetic Generation
The Man in the Sycamore Tree

MOUNT MARY COLLEGE LIBRARY
Milwaukee, Wisconsin 53222

Mother India's Children

Meeting Today's Generation in India

by EDWARD RICE / *Friendship Press*
Orbis Books

73-2438

1972

Copyright © 1971 by Edward Rice

All rights reserved under International
and Pan-American Copyright Conventions.
Published in the United States by Pantheon Books,
a division of Random House, Inc.,
and simultaneously in Canada by
Random House of Canada, Limited, Toronto.

TRADE NUMBER ISBN: 0-394-82036-3 GIBRALTAR NUMBER ISBN: 0-394-92036-3
Library of Congress Catalog Number: 75-138548
Designed by Janet Townsend
Manufactured in the United States of America

Paperback edition,
joint publishing venture of:
Friendship Press, New York, N.Y. and
Orbis Books, Maryknoll, New York,
by permission of the original publishers

915.4
R36

To Ted and Chris

The Children

Changing India

An Indian Lost, an Indian Gained

Mother India's Children and Mother India

Mother India's Children

Introduction

After I returned from my third trip to India, I had lunch with a friend. He asked me perfunctorily how I liked India. I tried to tell him what I had seen and experienced. I talked about the grandeur of India, the sweep of her history, the poverty and the riches, the failed opportunities and the rewards that were there for the taking, life and death, the tremendous scale of all things, from the crowds in the streets to the endless, vacant sky and the heat that strikes the brain like a bullet. He seemed to have tuned out, and muttered, like a litany, "India is obviously a land of contrasts." After he had said that for the fourth or fifth time, I changed the subject. India is too big to be absorbed in a single conversation, and even a single visit. One can easily fail India, and India can fail the individual, but the failure is that of one's own awareness. India cannot be approached on any but the most open terms. And that is what I have tried to do in the following pages, which are essentially the story of India, time past and time present and future, in the lives of some of her young people.

India is vast, but not so vast as one might expect. From one coast to the other, from Bombay on the West to Calcutta on the East, is only a distance of some 1,000 miles, though India extends further in the Northwest, and has a separate state, Assam, dangling by a thirteen mile corridor on the East, caught between Pakistan, Bhutan, Burma and mainland China. From the North, with the great Himalayan range of mountains where India shares a border with several countries (again including China), to the southern tip, with Ceylon, the serendipity island lying offshore, is about 2,250 miles. But within this area, large sections of which are uninhabitable, are well over half a billion people, probably more—about two and a half times the population of the United States, which has twice the land. India is the second most populous nation in the world, the first being mainland China. The World Health Organization has estimated that India will soon surpass China, and that these half billion people will triple their number in about 45 years. Yet this vast population is curiously limited in many ways. Only about a quarter of it (an optimistic estimate) has some schooling, and most of this group are men. The "literate" are something like 125,000,-000 people. But literacy is relative. A man who can sign his name might be called literate. The daily press has a circulation of only two and a half million, in all the Indian languages and English, from coast to coast and North to South. There are many western newspapers with such a circulation. India's weekly and monthly magazines have no bigger audience than the dailies. There is television in only one city, New Delhi, and hardly more than ten thousand sets. Radios are common, but batteries are expensive, and electrical current for table models is not always available. Many of India's half million villages have but a single radio.

Eighty percent of India lives in villages, whose primary contact is with other villages within a short radius. Country life is slow and timeless. Peasants follow the same methods of tilling and harvesting that their ancestors practiced two or three thousand years ago. Farm implements are still made of wood. Dietary and religious customs remain unchanged. The caste system—in which people are born into a certain rigid social group which strictly regulates their lives and allows no upward movement into a better life, and even exiles many people into a perpetual limbo where they are not permitted ordinary privileges like entering a temple—is still a dominant fact. Essentially India is the last of the great early civilizations—Hittite, Babylonian, Assyrian, Egyptian —to survive virtually unchanged. This is one of India's special characteristics, and one reason it is so fascinating.

The extreme poverty is like nothing you have ever seen or imagined. There is little comparable to it in America's city slums, bad as they are, or in the Appalachians or the deep South. A French traveler, Madeleine Biardeau remarked, "This frantic poverty, which will not let you rest, becomes an obsession once you have seen it at close range: you begin to understand why so many of the more privileged prefer to go on sleeping in peace."

But India is not a poor country. There is fantastic wealth: the rich are as rich as any in the West, with lands, factories, mines, businesses, jewels and art treasures that defy cataloging. There are great natural resources: water power, minerals, forests, fisheries. The land is said to be capable of supporting not one but two or three crops a year, given the proper seed and fertilizer. And India has one of the most powerful but under-used riches of all, a great labor force. One has only to see her peasants and factory hands at work to understand the tremendous potentiality that is yet to be used intelligently. The people are not lazy, except as their energy and creative abilities are sapped by undernourishment and disease. A farmer works from sunrise to sunset and longer with a steady unresting pace that few westerners can equal.

My encounters with the subjects of this book came about largely by chance. I wanted it to be so. After a short time in India one either flees or leaves things to kharma, to fate. One can lean on kharma to expedite the impossible, but I knew in advance that meetings would come about through the most tenuous circumstances. In some cases the details are explained in the book. One relaxes and lets the situation take over. Since India has seventeen major languages and several thousand dialects I often had to work through interpreters, in some cases through two languages (English into Hindi into another language and back). English is widely but inexpertly spoken, and tends to disappear entirely under pressure. I had brought a tape recorder and never used it. (At the end of this particular trip I received an offer from a black marketeer for it. There is a big demand for western and Japanese electronic equipment and cameras, but the standard price abroad is half of what Americans pay at home. Even the black market price in Bombay was less than what I had paid for my very good Japanese portable recorder in New York. So I brought it home.)

The conversations had little formal structure aside from the few pinpointing, warming-up questions for basic facts, like names, age (usually vague) and family background. One sits on the ground or the floor (in most cases) and lets events find their way. Often I would ask two rather esoteric questions. The first is one sometimes used by psychologists in America. It has three parts, and each part must be answered immediately without reflection. The first part is "Who are you?" The second is "Who are you?" As is the third. The unexpected repetition can lead the individual to a basic statement of his identity. I would always preface the question by saying that it was a kind of a game we sometimes play in America, just to prevent the subjects from a feeling of being pushed into a corner. I found that young Indians had a very definite sense of their own identity. On the other hand, while I was working on the book, I asked a middle-aged, unmarried, pretentious, pompous Indian businessman the same questions. He went to pieces and replied, "Nobody, oh nobody" to the first and refused any further answers. I've had the same reaction from some Americans who are not sure of their identities.

My other interest was their dream life. What does an Indian teenager dream about? I had no psychoanalytical motive. I was merely curious as to the content of the dreams of people in another culture. It would be foolish and irrelevant to try to put these dreams into a western Freudian context. Many, in fact, most Indians have no realization that they

6

dream. The concept had to be explained to them. In many cases the question was fruitless. In a few there were interesting answers which are reported in the appropriate chapters.

Some minor information. The Indian rupee is officially thirteen American cents, but its true rate of exchange is closer to ten. Even this, however, is only a sometime guide. Knowledgeable Indians will put the value of the rupee, in terms of buying labor or services or many commodities, at a dollar. Thus a man who earns five rupees a day (a good wage for an unskilled laborer) in effect is receiving five dollars a day—except that his pound of rice can cost one and a half to two rupees.

Traditional India

Keshav
Bhikaji Bendarkar

FISHERMAN, Age 13

There is an understood, unwritten axiom in India that every meeting tends to be a Cosmic Encounter. All assumes universal significance. The most casual passing becomes Cosmic, an Encounter. I remember sending a telegram from Darjeeling, the famous resort and tea capital in eastern India, to my son on his fifteenth birthday. He was then in school in Rhode Island. I wrote out his name and address and then a single word, NAMASTE, and signed it. It was getting dark and I had just time to slip into the telegraph office before it closed. The clerk at the counter took the telegram, counted the words, then read it. He read it several times. Meanwhile some other clerks were peering over his shoulder and they read the telegram. Someone remarked to me, "It is Indian word." I said, "Yes." "Do you know it is Indian word?" "Yes." Then we all discussed it, the clerks and me, the people standing in line behind me. This man, this foreigner, he is sending a telegram to his son in another country (few Indians really know about America; most have never heard of it) and his son knows Indian word. We may have discussed the subject for fifteen minutes. The people on line didn't object. It was a meeting of East and West, of time and space, the past and the present, all in cosmic dimensions, the mind and the telegraph machine clicking out without distinction an American teenager's name and address and the Indian message of peace. It seemed like an isolated incident, but on my next trip, when I was beginning this book, I recalled the Encounter when I set off to find the first young Indian to talk to.

I was in Bombay and had been trying without luck to get started. None of my friends seemed to know any young people except the most obviously westernized ones. Finally I was sent to a sociologist at Bombay University. I explained my purpose. He listened without seeming to hear what I was saying: I wanted to meet and talk to perhaps six teenagers in Bombay, a dozen in other cities and some in the countryside and even the jungle—about twenty to twenty-five in all. Could he introduce me to a few in Bombay? Dr. X interrupted me by asking, "How can you make a true statistical analysis with twenty-five? You need twenty-five hundred, five thousand, ten thousand. Thousands! How can you get a sample with twenty-five?" I said I didn't want a statistical sample; I wanted to talk to some young people to find out how they thought and what they felt and what it is like to grow up in India. Dr. X looked surprised. He didn't seem to believe that young people thought or felt. He told me to come back. I returned several times; often he wasn't in his office. Once he asked me to put my plan in writing, which I did, reluctantly and painfully because I wanted to develop the meetings on chance once they began, to be free, open, unstructured. Twice Dr. X had other sociologists with him. They couldn't believe I was going to do a book with only twenty-five teenagers. Why not twenty-five thousand? It would take years and a lot of money, they would offer their services (at a price, I assumed), but one must have a true statistical sample! It was a Cosmic Encounter that had gone wrong. They were adamant; I was adamant. Finally I gave up. I said so and

hypocritically gave Dr. X and his associates my heartfelt thanks. As I
was leaving, Dr. X said casually, "Oh, why don't you see my very dear
friend Dr. Gaokar." He gave me Dr. Gaokar's address and I saw him
the next morning.

"You are doing what we should be doing," said Dr. G. K. Gaokar. He
is a small, wiry man, with intense piercing eyes and a keen interest in
people. He is director of the social education center in a small section of
Bombay called Adarshnagar. "Last week we had terrible riots in Bombay—all over the city. Most of the people involved were teenagers,
some of them from this area, and we have no idea what they think they
were doing. I doubt that anyone has talked to a teenager. We don't
know what our own children are like." Dr. Gaokar and his assistant,
Mrs. Sudha Pandit, said they would find two or three young people for
me to talk to.

The next day I return and am told that a boy in a fishing village nearby
has agreed to see me. He is seventeen and is said to be bright. He
doesn't show up at the center, so I return again the following morning.
There is still no sign of the fisherman, and finally Mrs. Pandit suggests
that I go to the village, which is about a mile away, by foot. She sends
with me a young man who speaks some English, but not enough for me
to get an idea of really where we are going or of what is to be done. We
pass through a recently completed housing development which already
shows signs of the rigors of the tropics—plaster and paint are chipping
and peeling, there are water stains down the walls—and then past a
group of woven bamboo huts which house the desperately poor. We
cross an open area and enter Worli, a true Indian village with narrow
streets and old stone houses. My guide stops at a house. Some young
men join him; we stop again and again, picking up other people and
losing some. Everyone tries his English on me. Theirs is shaky and I am
annoyed at myself for not having studied Hindi—the national, all-
purpose language—as hard as I should have when I had the chance. We
pass through Worli village, through the rutted streets, through the
fish peddlers and the women going to the pump for water, through the
naked children and the sacred cows and the old people who smile ten-

tatively. It is now high noon and the sun is burning. I had been carrying a heavy camera case but several people have struggled for the honor of carrying it for me. A few hundred yards on the sea-ward side of Worli is a small hill with the ruins of an old church and a fort. Worli had once been a Portuguese outpost. Later the Portuguese lost Bombay (the name means good bay in Portuguese) to the English and the land between Worli and Bombay, which is also an island, was filled in. We clamber along some jutting black rocks to the point. Some fishing boats have just come over the horizon. A few have motors and arrive very quickly. Three boats pull into the shore and fishermen jump out with wooden half-barrels of small pink fish. "Where is the boy I am to talk to?" I ask repeatedly. "Oh, he is here, sir," my guides tell me. "Yes, but which one?" "Oh, he is here, sir." I want to photograph the boy and his crew as they unload their boat. "Now we go sir," say my guides after an hour. "Yes, but where is the boy?" "Oh, he has come and gone, sir." I feel immensely frustrated and slightly angry at all the confusion, but everyone else is in a good mood and pleased at having shown the foreigner the fishing boats. They ask me to take their picture and line up along the shore, standing stiffly, like a row of soldiers.

Then we begin to walk towards the fort. There is a tiny figure on the skyline, straightening out a net to dry. "Is that the boy?" "Yes, that is boy." We approach the boy, my eleven guides and I and some fishermen and young children who have tagged along. The boy looks up. He would have run if he could but we have suddenly surrounded him. My guides begin to pound him with questions. We are standing in the open in the full fury of the sun. "It's too hot here," I say, "let's go into the fort." The roof has fallen in but we squat in the shade of a wall. Everyone is talking at once. Finally there is some quiet. I feel completely lost about where to begin. "What is the boy's name?" There is a flurry of conversation. "He say, Keshav Bhikaji Bendarkar." It takes a few minutes for me to get it spelled correctly. "How old is the boy?" More conversation. "Twelve," says someone without asking the boy. "Ask him when he will be thirteen." A long flurry of conversation. "He is thirteen now, sir." The boy is small, fine boned and looks healthy; he is shy but eager to please.

I am a fisherman. So is my father. He works on the same boat I do, but he also has his own boat and goes out on that. This is my first year of fishing. We come from Navnagar village in Dabole [up the coast from Bombay]. I have never been to school. We fish seven days a week, morning and night. It is best by moonlight. We—that is my family, my brother fishes too—earn thirty rupees a day, depending on how the fish are running. We are members of the Kharvi caste [a subcaste of the Sudras, the lowest. I am told by the others that all fishermen are Kharvis, which I know isn't so]. Fishing is our life. I haven't been to Bombay, only to Worli. I am a poor man. I have never seen a movie, but sometimes I hear the radio. A lot of people have transistors. I like to sing, movie songs, things like that [but he refuses to sing now, being very shy]. On Holi I put red powder on my face. That is my life.

Several days prior to this, I had drawn up a long list of questions: his work, education, future, his opinions, general knowledge, politics, his views of India, America, Pakistan, China, the world, space, student demonstrations, his hopes, fears, his own position in the complex social strata of his country. But virtually everything is irrelevant. He knows nothing of India, he has had no education. He has had no experiences. An American teenager would have been full of opinions, ideas, information, suggestions. I am face to face with peasant India. Keshav is all of peasant India, the poor man who exists, survives, who lives and dies with scarcely a ripple on the surface. He tells me he will marry at twenty-one. "Why twenty-one?" I ask. My guides say that twenty-one is the government rule; it is not, it is only a suggestion, late marriage in order to try to slow down the birth rate.

Keshav has nothing but his immediate life, the sea. There is nothing to look forward to but the same. "I am a poor man." He is India. Not far away I am to find a girl who is his counterpart.

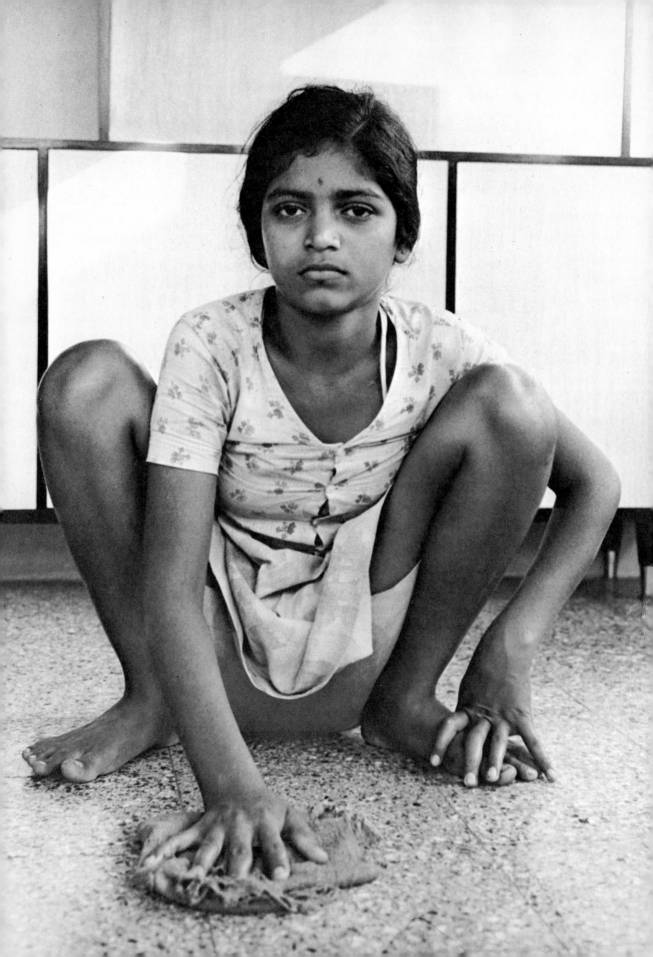

MOUNT MARY COLLEGE LIBRARY
Milwaukee, Wisconsin 53222

Lata
Sakharam Narvankar

SWEEPER, Age 12

Lata Sakharam Narvankar is all too typical of millions of India's desperately poor working class people. Her life is restricted to an unending round of work, poverty, and scraping by with hardly enough to eat. She was born into a world that always works: children begin to work as soon as they can toddle. They have simple jobs to do. When the next baby is born, an older one, either a boy or a girl, finds it his responsibility to care for the baby. It is common to see a five-year-old child with a younger one on the hip, and at the same time holding the hand of a two-year-old. Then there are other jobs, cooking and cleaning, drawing water, buying a handful of rice or vegetables. Children who live in business and tourist areas beg. There are very few childhood games, no toys, no schooling, no entertainment (such as movies) except

19

73-2438

for the frequent religious and popular festivals. At best, the poor can listen to someone else's transistor radio. Their lives are limited. But this is not to dismiss the poor and their children offhandedly. After seeing large numbers of them, and talking to a few, I always got the impression of a great interior nobility.

Lata and her family live in a hutment, in the northern part of the city of Bombay, a few hundred yards from the rocky shore that faces the Indian Ocean. During the day one can see the large lumbering fishing boats, the *dhows,* that come down from Bandra, a fishing village that now has been swallowed up by Bombay's growth. About six blocks away from the hutment is the main thoroughfare that runs through the city, called at this point Dr. Annie Besant Road, after the noted theosophist and mystic. But Lata rarely sees either the ocean or the road. Her life is polarized between the apartment where she works as a domestic and the one-room thatched hut where her family lives. The hutment, one of the most abject kinds of tenement housing, is made of woven palm leaves, loose enough to let in a few breezes at night, if there are any. The roof is thatch. The sun beats down relentlessly. In the summer monsoon, when the rain falls in heavy sheets, everything is wet and damp, and the water runs in streams through the narrow unpaved streets, carrying refuse and excrement along with it. There are colonies of hutments all over the city.

I came across Lata through Mrs. Pandit at the center for young working class people. The center is about a quarter of a mile from Lata's hutment and within sight of the housing development where she works. We had some difficulty in meeting: Lata didn't really believe that a foreigner wanted to talk to her, but finally one hot afternoon we met at last. The sun streamed down through the windows of the center, baking everything.

Mrs. Pandit had remarked that it would be interesting to talk to a sweeper girl because she spends her day in the middle class world and her nights in the world of the poor. "Lata goes from comfort to poverty" said Mrs. Pandit to me. "Poverty" is the key word, because it is not only a physical poverty, but a poverty of experience and knowledge as well, tempered only by that innate interior beauty. But one can see that the beauty will remain static, and could eventually shrivel and die, as clearly had happened in the case of her parents. They are wretched and uninspired. Her father is an industrial worker in the dyeing department of a Bombay mill. Her mother is a sad, gentle woman with liquid eyes and a humble manner. She is ill and rarely works. The burden of supporting the family falls upon Lata and her father.

I have brought along as translator an upper-middle-class Indian woman named Miss Lakshmi Lal, who is quite hip to the West. She reads *Vogue,* belongs to a film club which shows movies which are otherwise banned in India, dresses in high fashion (Indian) and has just bought a very fine book on Henry Moore's sculpture, which, we are to find out, cost the equivalent of eight months' wages for Lata. Miss Lal is slightly apprehensive when I first bring her to the center, but after several trips she begins to accept it.

Early every morning, six days a week (seven if necessary) Lata goes to the apartment of a middle class family in the housing development adjoining the hutments. She says the family is nice—she wouldn't admit to anything else—and during the day she is allowed to listen to the radio as she works. She prefers music from the Hindi films, a minor-key, sadly lilting series of songs about unrequited love and paramours seen in the distance, or about the approaching end of life, or sometimes about a wedding or the sorrow of existence in a cruel world—almost all subjects that touch upon her own life.

> I work for a family from Gujerat. I have three sisters and a brother. He is twenty but is unemployed. It's very hard getting a job in Bombay. All those people come in from the villages looking for work, and then people like my brother, who was born here, cannot get a job. My father works in the dyeing department at Century Mills. My mother has asthma. Sometimes she works as a sweeper but she is really not very well. We are originally from Colaba, which is on the other side of the city. What do I do? I am a sweeper. Which means that I do washing, cleaning, swabbing, sweeping, some of the shopping. I bring rice to the mill to have it ground. I speak Marathi, Hindi, Sindi, and Gujarati. Wherever I work I

pick up the language. There are so many families that come from outside the city. I'm earning twenty-one rupees a month. I stay here all the time, right here, where I work, or home or sometimes I come to the center for sewing lessons. No, I haven't been to Bombay [she means the downtown area]. I haven't seen a movie, but I once rode in a taxi. It was, well, a long time ago. But I remember the taxi. I haven't seen a movie because I have no money. I give my pay to my Mum. Twenty-one rupees a month. My Mum makes my clothes.

[Miss Lal asks her some questions.] America? That must be another town. China? Pakistan? Other towns, I guess. I stay in Bombay. Mrs. Gandhi? No, I never heard of her.

She has small bones, her eyes look tired, and though she is only thirteen there are premature wrinkles around them. Basically she is a very beautiful girl, and a naturally intelligent one, but the social structure has already limited her. She is frozen into a way of life that offers no outlet and no future. In fact, she does not think about the future. It requires persistent questioning to force her mind towards the years ahead. She thinks very little about anything: she has blocked off her mind because so much is unobtainable and her primary concerns are to please the woman she works for and her parents. The moment rather than the past or the future is her preoccupation.

How long will she work, I wonder. And when will she marry? Miss Lal translates. Lata buries her face in her hands and giggles. Miss Lal keeps questioning gently. "Next year?" "No." "When you are eighteen?" "No." "Twenty, twenty-two?" "Yes." This seems very late, but we can't get it clear. What occurs to us later is that for a thirteen-year-old sweeper girl with no education, twenty-two is a euphemism for "someday" or "whenever my parents wish it." What the foreigner rarely realizes is that the illiterate poor of the Third World have no sense of time, no calendar except general events, like "the year of the great monsoon," or "the year the baby died." Lata's "twenty-two" means "in the future."

Miss Lal asks, "What would you do if you had all the money you wanted?" Lata looks confused. This is an idea so far-fetched and crazy that it had never entered her mind. There is a long silence. Lata thinks she would like some food. Miss Lal offers some suggestions. "Buy clothes?" Yes, Lata would like some clothes. Like most children in Indian cities she wears a western dress (at eighteen she will wear a sari). "Go to the movies?" Lata had never thought of seeing a movie. The possibility has been so remote she could not even daydream about it. There are no daydreams in her life. Finally she says "Yes." But basically, we can see that there is nothing she craves. She can't imagine that there are things to be bought, to be enjoyed, that there are luxuries, or even that she would ever pass beyond the starvation line. There is nothing in her life except work, the next meal, a dry place in the monsoon, a simple dress to cover her nakedness with, the chance to hear the sad Hindi songs on her employer's radio.

Miss Lal and I follow Lata to her job. Her mistress is a very shy, kindly woman who stays in the next room while I photograph Lata washing the floor. Lata and her sister, who has tagged along, go to the mill to have some rice ground and Miss Lal and I walk over to the hutment. Lata and the sister run ahead to tell the family we are coming. The path—it can not be called a street—is rutted and filled with garbage and excrement. A few chickens scatter before us and the pariah dogs look up lazily. Lata's family is awaiting us and looking anxious. Her father's face is tired, her mother is tired, and her brother, who cannot find work, is wan and depressed. Lata, for the day, is a celebrity, and the neighbors crowd around to look at not only the foreign gentleman but the rich Indian lady who have visited the hutments. There is a lot of milling about, people crowding into the hutment. It is the end of the day and the air is still. The heat grows worse. Finally Miss Lal and I, after profuse goodbyes, walk back through the muddy street, through the naked children, the chickens and the lazy dogs. We find a taxi and go to downtown Bombay, where we have tea in a large air-conditioned dining room with yards of gleaming white cloth on tables served by obsequious barefoot servants in turbans. Miss Lal seems somewhat shaken and distracted. "I should take that child to a movie," she says.

Raj Bala

BRAHMIN FARM WIFE, Age 17

On India's great plain the villages change imperceptibly: some are larger or smaller, richer or poorer. The architecture varies slowly, according to the available materials: mud, stone, wattle, bamboo. The villages are likely to be run on a loose feudal system, dominated by two or three families, usually Brahmins, who also control the *panchayat,* the village council which is the guiding force and the local government. No one disputes their role. In many villages, where nine out of ten people depend on the land, these ruling Brahmin families control about half of it. In numerous cases the villages are fragmented by a duplication of such necessary things as ponds and wells, temples, and even roads, because each caste, or group of castes, has its own and does not share them with others. Life exists on a number of levels. Sometimes the caste groups are intertwined, performing services or working for each other. On various occasions they follow separate paths, with different celebrations of the same festival (Hindu priests will serve only higher caste families), or different festivals entirely, depending on the caste and the strictness of their orthodoxy.

Raj Bala, the daughter of a well-to-do Brahmin farmer, lives in a village that might be any of the tens of thousands on the northern plain. Her family is well off and has a large house—a complex of stone and mud buildings centered around a large courtyard where an ox stands drowsily wondering what to do, and a solid-wheel cart and a broken wooden plough await repairs. The village is about half a mile from a main road used by trucks and buses. From time to time there is a broken down bus which will connect with another that goes into New Delhi. Even though the road is asphalt, it is dusty. A boy walks by with a cow. He is holding on to the tail, a common practice. The cow's tail is twisted to make it move. The result is that nearly every cow has a kinked, broken tail. Then a herd appears, moving rapidly. The herdsmen walk in long swinging strides, either twisting tails or poking the cows with slim switches from saplings to make them hurry. The trees lining the road are already withered, the crops in the fields are scraggly and only knee-high because the rains have not yet come. Heat and dust: the inevitable combination.

I have come by bus from New Delhi, a precarious trip. I had been told by my contact, a Miss Pravesh Sharma, to take the bus to Tilaknagar; I would find it outside the Regal Theatre in the center of the city. This turns out to be very vague. There are buses going in two directions outside the Regal, and I finally find what I think is my bus a few blocks away. The signs are in Devanagari script—there are a few characters I never learned—but someone assures me this is the right bus. We ride for a long time. The bus is crowded with people coming or going, with fruit and vegetables, animals, bed rolls, children; everyone is jammed together like on a New York subway. The passengers are shyly friendly and look at me out of the corners of their eyes. All of them are frightfully poor. Finally the bus comes to a full stop and empties out. I get out too, not knowing if I have missed Miss Sharma,

but there she is, and we get into another bus and at last we are let off
in the middle of a plain. There is a tea shop on one side of the road and
in the distance, up a dirt road, is the village shimmering in the morning
heat. It is called Nawada. As we approach the village Miss Sharma puts
the free end of her sari over her head because the villagers are very con-
servative and it would be improper for her to be seen by the men with
her head uncovered.

The interior of the Balas' house is cool. Thirty-three people live
here, eighteen adults and fifteen children. The young ones run all over,
uninhibited. The little boys are completely naked, the girls wear a loose
shirt and nothing else. Raj Bala is sitting on a cot in a large entrance
room talking to her brothers' wives. Her mother enters, refreshed and
cheerful after bathing. She has just come from the pond; Indians have
a ritual bath after defecating (very early in the morning, if it is possible)
and may enjoy additional baths during the day. Raj and the brothers'
wives drop on the floor and kiss her feet and then run their hands up
and down the lower part of her legs in a kind of supplicating gesture.
Every woman who enters the room does this while I am there. She is
the matriarch.

Raj is taller and better fed than most Indians, who are small and
thin (one study reported that the average Indian farmer weighs less
than a hundred pounds and his wife about eighty-five). She has a beautiful smile and light skin. She wears a baggy kind of trouser called the
salwar and a tunic called the *kurta* and keeps a scarf, the *dupatta,*
around her head. This is a type of dress common in northern India,
West Pakistan, and Afghanistan. (The sari is really a southern style.)
Raj is charming and begins to show some self-possession as we talk. It
is very unusual for an Indian woman of almost any caste or group to
talk to a strange man, especially in a village. But she seems pleased that
she has been chosen.

> We have just got television in Nawada. There are not many sets in
> India. The station is in New Delhi and the government is putting
> a set in each village in order to inform and educate the people. It's
> a good idea. We have programs three times a week at night, mostly

educational subjects like farming, and some documentary programs on other countries. That's why I know about America. (My brothers have told me something, too.) You send us food. And the moon landing and so on. You are a rich country, but oh so noisy and crowded! I'd like to visit America but I think I'd be a little bit afraid, too. We have one television set, in the building where the *panchayat* meets, and we sit around in the open and watch it.

We are Brahmins and one of the leading families in Nawada. There are seventeen kinds of Brahmins, but I don't know which type we are. It depends on the locality. There are other kinds of Brahmins in other parts of India. Brahmins don't eat meat at all. No Brahmin could. No Hindu should, though some people in the lower castes are said to. I went to school before I was married and learned some English. We speak Hindi here—it's our national language—but English is important. My brothers can speak English.

The ring on my toe means I am married. My husband's name is Sabtir Sharma [he is not related to Miss Sharma]. In some parts of India a married woman wears a large metal collar, but here it is a ring on the second toe. [This is a practice adopted by many western hippie girls in India; they go barefoot. I doubt that they know the significance of the toe ring.] I was married when I was thirteen. That's when most girls are married. [The marriage was arranged by the couple's parents. Raj and Sabtir did not see each other until the day of their marriage. When I ask her what she thought of him at first sight, she giggles and covers her face with her hands.] Oh, he was so handsome! He's tall and has a nice smile. We were married four years ago. [Find out when it was consummated, I suggest to Miss Sharma. She looks startled, but asks. Raj giggles, looks flustered and covers her face with her hands. I am not sure I am going to get an answer, and I cannot find out how Miss Sharma, who is a very shy and gentle woman, is phrasing the question. But she reports: "It was consummated a year ago." Raj stops giggling and straightens up.]

We are all Brahmins, Sabtir and I and our families. Brahmins have to marry Brahmins. We cannot marry other castes. [A look of

horror crosses her face when I ask this question.] In fact, I think inter-caste marriages are wrong. You cannot mix the castes. And no Hindu can marry a Muslim or a foreigner. That's wrong, too. We cannot eat meat or eggs.

Now I work in the fields with my brothers and their wives. We grow wheat, grain, barley and maize. We don't eat rice here. The basic diet is wheat. We make flat cakes called *chappatis* out of wheat and water and then we have vegetables and spices. Sometimes I go to Delhi to stay with my uncle for the festivals (but he won't let me go to the movies). There are so many: *diwali,* the feast of lights, and *holi,* when we throw colored water and powder on each other, and the swing festival. We have dances and processions. Sometimes I go to Rotak, which is nearer than Delhi, to see Sabtir. Sabtir is studying there. Sabtir's family are farmers but he would like to go into civil service. He could earn good money, about three hundred rupees a month, though if he is unlucky it would be as little as a hundred and fifty. What will happen is that he will get a job in the city after he graduates and I will live with his family until he sends for me. His family is not far away. When he is on holiday I stay with Sabtir in his father's house. I will always be able to come back here to see my parents.

Someday I would like to go to America. You know, many people have never heard about it. We were told about America in school and we have had some American agricultural experts in Nawada. I don't think I'd mind living there, though the noise might frighten me. We get food from America and farm equipment. It's a big country and helps my country. The people are nice. Loveable.

I would like to have some children after Sabtir graduates. I think three would be an ideal number because that is what the government asks us to have, no more. The government is headed by a woman—I can't remember her name—but the people are being requested not to have too many children. If we ever go to America it would be interesting to see how the young people live. They have a much different life from mine. They lead a good life. There are good facilities—clean, modern, and a lot of liberty, education, food, a high standard of living—all very good things. The young people can go out of their own will, according to their own choice. This doesn't mean I approve completely. The young people should consult their parents first. But as I said, the people are nice and loveable.

I had a dream last night about Sabtir [she becomes flustered]. I was sitting beside him, talking, and then we went for a walk in the fields . . .

Shyam Narayam Tidori

GURU, *Age 17*

When I met Shyam Narayam Tidori I felt for the first time in my life that I was in the presence of ancient man. He is a guru, a spiritual guide, whose calling is to incorporate the highest values a Hindu may look for in any man. Shyam is seventeen, yet he already has disciples. Without a guru, no man can become a twice-born or caste Hindu. When a young man is initiated into Hinduism, it is the guru who gives him the sacred thread and whispers into his ear the *mantra,* or sacred verse, he will keep secret for the rest of his life. A guru never looks for disciples: they come to him. Neo-Hindu westerners who establish themselves as gurus advertise for disciples as if they had something to sell. It is the opposite in India. Some gurus may be only village priests, but others are true saints in the great tradition of Indian spirituality. Without a guru a man can never hope to reach *mukti,* or salvation. It is a difficult path, attaining *mukti,* and the guru's aim is not to teach certain doctrines but to transpose his disciple's whole being to a different plane of existence.

The background of the guru, his way of life, his education, theology, philosophy and practical knowledge are drawn from long studies of the *Vedas,* four collections of very ancient works which deal not only with religious and philosophical themes, but also with rituals and ceremonies and rites, medicine, astronomy, phonetics, philology and grammar. They include hymns, poetry, chants and magic conjurations. *Veda* means essentially "knowledge" and as far as anyone can guess— all is very hazy in the remote past—they began to assume form about four thousand years ago. Originally they were passed down orally through rigid, extremely accurate mnemotechnic methods. The Vedic peoples of India had a common origin with the Celts, Greeks, Latins, Germans, Slavs, Armenians, Georgians and the tribes of Central Asia. Co-equal with them were the Hittites, Babylonians, Persians, Assyrians and the Jews of the Bible.

Shyam comes from a village called Dhamauli, which has five hundred inhabitants. He is studying at Sanskrit University in Benares. The University is a beautiful pink gothic building constructed under the British raj. Today it is no longer an outpost of England, but a vestige of Vedic India.

> We are gurus, that is priests and teachers, my father and his father and my brothers and I, as far back as anyone can remember. We are priests by heredity. Brahmins, the priestly caste. We are the face of Brahman, the Absolute, the One Reality which is the Ground and Principle of all beings.
>
> At the present time I am studying astronomy and medicine, and Sanskrit. I will spend seven years on my courses: two on astronomy because that is the basis for predicting horoscopes, and five on medicine. Sanskrit is necessary because it is the language of the Vedas. Traditional Indian medicine is different from western. It is ayurvedic and is the system taught by the Vedas from the earliest

days. This is the science of herbs and plants and certain prayers which restore people to health. We have great faith in them. I began studying Sanskrit at age eleven. Not only are the sacred books written in it, but also those on astronomy and medicine.

[What he would do for a patient with a fever?] If we were in my village, I would observe the symptoms and consult the books to see what should be done. We can tell by the type of fever and how the patient looks—his eyes and pulse and general appearance—what should be done. In a typical fever case I would take the leaves of a plant called tulsi—it's holy to the Lord God Vishnu—and grind them into a powder along with a small sheet of black paper and boil the powder in water with some salt and sugar according to the patient's taste. He will be cured by this. [He couldn't answer when I asked him about a broken leg; his studies hadn't reached that point.]

[What is a guru? He cracks his fingers and thinks. Shyam has uncommonly long pauses between sentences. I am forcing him to analyze and codify things which he accepts as experience. I am being western and rational, methodical; he is being Hindu and experiential. One does not define what "is."]

A guru bestows *diksha*—initiation—for the welfare of human beings. It is a sacred act, a kind of sacrament, which a guru gives a man after he has reached the age of eighteen and is married. If someone is ill he can take *diksha*. [What is *diksha?* He scratches himself and there is another exceptionally long pause.] First of all, the client obtains a full set of clothing for the guru—a colored safron *dhoti*, a *kurta* or shirt, a *chaddha* or shawl and a *gummcha* or scarf. He also gives the guru certain utensils—a copper water pot, a metal glass [glass is now the Hindi word], a bowl and a dish. Later he gives money too. The central act of the ceremony comes when the guru covers his head and the disciple's with a scarf and puts his mouth to the other man's ear and chants the sacred *mantra*. One *mantra* goes like this: OM RAM RAMAYANA. This is chanted five times. [Some *mantras* consist of unintelligible nonsensical Sanskrit words.] Then the client invites his neighbors to

his house in celebration. The guru always stays overnight. A Brahmin who has received *diksha* can pass it on to other people.

My father gives *diksha* since he is a guru. He is also a farmer. He has fifteen acres of land and grows winter wheat, barley, gram, peas and monsoon crops like rice. My wife is staying at his house now. We were married this year. I didn't see her until the day of the marriage. Her father is a teacher of Sanskrit at Ayodha, one of the seven sacred cities. I'll be both a guru and a doctor, and I'll have a farm too. I'll have servants to help me with the field work. But whatever I do, I am first of all a guru, a Brahmin, and must perform my priestly duties.

My special devotion is to the Lord God Shiva. He looks after my welfare. Shiva is [there is a very long silence] . . . is . . . Shiva is a god who is very quickly propitiated, he is easily pleased, he responds quickly. His name means "benevolent." [I want to know how he envisions Shiva.] I see him as an idol, as an idol in the temple. He is always the same, wherever you go. The proportions of the idol are exactly regulated in the *Shilpa Shastras*.

I go to the temple to pray daily, morning and evening both. The prayer is the *Sloka*. In the morning I offer water—it is poured on the idol—and leaves from the bel tree. In the evening I light small lamps (we use ghee as fuel) and place them around the idol.

[I am curious about re-incarnation.] After death, according to one's *kharma*—evil, sin or good—a man goes into a different womb. There are eighty-four *lakhs,* cycles, of life [a *lakh* is 100,000] —bird, animal, man and so on. There is a circle of life and death: it never stops, it goes on forever. By virtuous deeds in sufficient number a man goes to heaven, and gets eternal rest. [What is heaven like?] Heaven is a place which, once attained, the soul does not want to leave. The soul is freed from all sorts of worldly boundaries.

All people have the same kind of soul, rich, poor, high or low caste. The caste system is man-made. A child comes from God. All people are created equal, all must go through the same cycle of life and death. It is immaterial whether you are Hindu or Christian.

There is a very long silence. He picks up his battered, rusty bicycle which has been leaning against a wall. We each bow and make the *namaste,* and he rides off on the bicycle, which at the moment looks not the least bit contemporary but like an ancient ritual object unearthed from one of the long buried Vedic civilizations of the Indus valley.

Radia Begum

MUSLIM GIRL, Age 13

Radia Begum (literally Miss Radia—she has no family name) is thirteen. She is big and has large hands; she is larger than her brother who is fifteen and very active and outspoken. She has long eyelashes and the classical features one sees in Indian miniature paintings. But she constantly keeps her eyes down, not looking even at other women when they address her. Her grandfather was a taxi driver, her father owns a small factory. The family lives in a tightly packed middle class section of Bombay known as Kemp's Corner. One of her neighbors, a woman named Sharma Godwani, introduced me, after we had spent days negotiating with Radia's mother for a meeting. Miss Godwani gave me periodic reports about progress in getting together. It seemed so vague that I was constantly tempted to abandon my attempt to talk to a "traditional" young Muslim girl. As a minority in a very powerful Hindu nation, Muslims are reluctant to do anything that might attract attention—that is how they feel, anyway—and on top of that we had to overcome the traditional shyness of the Muslim woman. Miss Godwani was never sure that she had made contact with Radia's mother. In India, people who don't want to do something rarely say no. There is a kind of tuning out, a drifting away and a vagueness that one can never cope with. Communication ceases. But after a number of frustrating delays Miss Godwani brought us all together.

It is a larger group than I had expected. Miss Lal has come to help with language difficulties, and Radia appears with her brother and her parents (the mother and father eventually go downstairs to their apartment) and her "uncle," a man named Hakim Syed Akbar, who claims to be a relative—"Oh, Radia Begum is just like a daughter to me. She grew up on my lap"—but is eventually revealed as just a neighbor who has forced himself upon us as a chaperone. The afternoon starts off poorly. Whenever I ask Radia Begum a question, Hakim Syed Akbar answers. If I speak to her brother, the Hakim answers. And if I speak to Miss Lal or Miss Godwani, he tries to answer. I suppose that he is answering for me too. The conversation bounces around in Urdu and Hindi and various shades of English. When Radia Begum is finally persuaded to speak, her voice is so soft and faint that no one can hear her. I suggest that we turn off the fan. It is intensely hot and our soft drinks have quickly risen to room temperature. After the fan is turned off everyone sits melting, with energy levels dropping rapidly. Finally, to get into a real conversation with Radia Begum, I request that everyone go away, leaving me with Radia and either Miss Lal or Miss Godwani. Since Miss Lal has already had some experience in working with me she stays. But I realize that the Hakim has not really gone. He is standing outside the door to the hall, behind a curtain. I see his sandaled feet underneath, shifting back and forth. Every once in a while, he interjects an answer through the curtain, though not quite daring to rush back into the room. In some ways the conversation with Radia Begum never develops, but in other ways it is quite illustrative

of the manner in which Muslim women have been treated in the Islamic world, even in India. They have no freedom and alternate between the confines of rigid custom and the whims of their families.

> I just gave up the *bourkha*. I don't think that women should be veiled. That is something out of the past. We are free today. My mother was upset, but she agreed. We are living in a modern world.
>
> I go to Islamic Girls School, which is half an hour away by bus. It's Urdu medium but we also learn Hindi and English and I speak Marathi too. My special friends are Nessim and Abida.
>
> My family came from Kerala state. There are many Muslims there, along the coast. I was born in Bombay. I haven't been out of the city. On Sundays we sometimes go to a museum or to the zoo. I don't have any close friends here—they're all at school. At home I help my mother with the cooking. We have wheat, rice, meat and fish, and I help with the other children. We sometimes have movies in school, but I've never been to a movie theatre.
>
> My father has a small factory. He makes light parts for motors. He has four or five men working for him.
>
> My favorite subjects? Languages. Urdu and Marathi. I like the Urdu poets [but she will not recite them for us].

This has taken about an hour, these few facts. Miss Lal asks her what she would like to do after school, marry or go to college. Radia Begum sits with her head down and her eyes lowered for a long time without speaking. Miss Lal questions her gently. Finally Radia Begum says she doesn't want to go to college but will marry if that is what the family desires. When she is seventeen she will marry the man they find for her. That is what she wants.

Miss Lal to me: "I think she really means it the other way around. She'd prefer to go to college. I'm sure of it. That old idiot in the hall is going to report everything she says to her parents."

Miss Lal continues her gentle questioning. Radia Begum says she doesn't go to the mosque but prays at home. "Who are you?" A long pause. "A Muslim woman." The second question brings complete silence, a long silence. Obviously the answer will never come. Her mother and father pass in and out. The mother is bigger than the father. The brother comes and remarks, "Oh, she's very shy, even with friends. She never says anything. But at home she laughs and talks."

Miss Godwani comes back and turns on the fans. I want to take some photographs of Radia. Miss Godwani has to go downstairs to negotiate with the mother. The message comes back: "No photographs." "In the *bourkha?*" I ask. Another trip downstairs. "No, not even in the *bourkha.*" However it is clear that Radia Begum is quite pleased at the idea of being photographed, though she covers her face with her hands. We finally talk her into putting her hands on her lap. She sits with her eyes cast to the floor. "See if you can get some reaction from her," I ask both Miss Lal and Miss Godwani. They try, asking questions and chattering back and forth in small talk, but Radia Begum shows no sign of interest in the conversation and won't answer further questions. She still sits with her eyes cast toward the floor. Then we go out on the balcony. There are children running in the street. Big black crows battle with each other. Music is pouring out of radios, each tuned to a different station. In the distance we hear the roar of cars crashing through Kemp's Corner. Miss Godwani tries to get Radia Begum to respond— to laugh, to smile, to frown, to look up, to react to the world around her. But Radia Begum is determined. A Muslim woman remains passive and subservient before a strange man.

Omprakash Thirani

ENGINEERING STUDENT, Age 19

Benares: at dawn the sun comes up over the Ganges, a white dot in the blue-gray sky, like a hole punched in a tremendous sheet of dark paper. Suddenly the dot disappears and the sky is flooded with light and heat. All along the north shore of the river pilgrims gingerly climb down the steep stone steps, the *ghats,* into the gently flowing murky water. Holy men sit under thatched palm umbrellas in meditation. Going south along the Ganges one comes to a huge sprawling campus arranged in a half-circle. This is Benares Hindu University, a rambling collection of colleges and graduate schools which are the pride of Indian education. There are schools for the various disciplines, and students come from all over the world. There are thousands of girls too, the best of Indian society, who, to be frank

(and some Indians will talk about it in a bitter joking manner) are at the University merely to get a degree so they can attract a better type of husband. One girl remarked, "When all the boys are looking for educated girls, where will my parents find me a decent boy?" And then there are the girls whose parents have been unable to find a proper husband at all and use the university as one way of keeping busy. But for young men, education is a far more serious proposition. For many it represents a considerable financial sacrifice, though even a degree does not guarantee an adequate job. But for others, education is a way of spending a number of years in minor drudgery. I got the strong impression that Omprakash Thirani, a nineteen-year-old student at the University, is one of those who is sitting it out.

He is an Indian from Sikkim, one of the three small states in the Himalayas on India's northern border. His family moved to Sikkim for business reasons. There are many Indians in the small states and so strong is Indian influence that they are virtually colonies, much as they resist the idea. Unfortunately for the well-being of these states, they are landlocked and the only other neighbors are Communist China or Pakistan.

Omprakash is an only child. His father died three months before his birth, but he is a member of a joint family of eighteen people, so he has not had a lonely childhood. He is now in the engineering school at the University. There are a lot of western hippies in Benares, many of them living in houseboats on the river. Omprakash, like virtually all Indians, is irritated by them.

> The general public doesn't like hippies at all. Indians have always respected white skins. Now they are losing their respect. A hippie will hire a rickshaw and won't pay. Nobody likes them. They're known as smugglers, they take LSD, they're mentally dissolute, they're not satisfied with their lives. It's frustration, the jet age, everything is so fast. There are no Indian hippies. Why does the West alone produce hippies? The West is more advanced, it has everything, yet it has hippies. I don't think India will ever have

hippies. A few people pose as hippies but they're not. We have a higher set of values and no one need be a hippie.

[I felt a certain resentment and sadness in his attitude. Indians are afraid of letting loose. They never admit to desires or attitudes that run counter to those generally accepted and imposed upon everyone.]

I'm in touch with students in the West. I write to some in France. They're all dominated by Communists. It's true here, too. Communism is a big failure. I'm personally against Communism. I don't appreciate Communist views. I'm not against the ideology of the Communist party, but it is not practical. I think I'd welcome a peaceful revolution—revolution through education. We do need a change of environment: it will take some time, it should happen. Perhaps I'm just a visionary.

Our students are restless. They're not satisfied with the educational system. Violence is the most popular manner of protesting here. Raise the fees and the students strike. Politicians excite the students. In any country, the politicians' fundamental aim is to create chaos. Mrs. Gandhi has kept things under control. I like her. Good or bad, she's got a strong policy. The rest of the cabinet suffers from a personality cult.

There was an article in an Australian magazine about coeducational dormitories. I don't believe in such activities. We are quite orthodox in our thinking, though we are getting more freedom nowadays. It is becoming quite common to have intercaste marriages. Arranged marriages are no longer necessary, but they are very much preferred, and they are happier. I think they prevent divorce and remarriage. We do have dating. A few years ago it was socially reprehensible, but now we date singly or in groups. If you have a constant girl there is a seventy-five percent chance it will lead to marriage, most often with family approval if the boy and girl are from the same caste. But intercaste marriages in a situation like this, no.

I've had a very novel idea. It has to do with family planning and population. The poor in India have more children than the rich. I believe in mass sterilization of the poor. It will cut down on their number. There may be a revolution over it, but if we want to remove poverty we've got to do it. But India is not all poverty. There are many good things which are being ignored. We've had some real progress. America has its poor, too.

Family planning is the only solution. One or two children are sufficient. It's becoming more popular day by day, especially in the poorest areas.

But there are problems. We have this burning desire to go abroad. I think ninety percent of our students apply to foreign universities. Foreign exchange is the main difficulty. We can't pay our way, so we need scholarships. But so few can go.

Omprakash's thinking is turned inward and shows itself in a fear of anything that might threaten either his equilibrium or his definitely well-to-do way of life. As an engineering student he is training for a profession that has no great possibilities of employment, but he seems to have no worries about whether he will work or not. There are now about 60,000 unemployed engineers in India. Another student said that a short time ago there had been a strike by unemployed engineers: they wanted either work or a subsidy of 250 rupees a month. The situation, as is so usual in India, was not resolved.

Omprakash stood looking morosely at me, and I went down to walk along the sandy banks of the Ganges, where tens of thousands of people were silently bathing and praying.

City India

Jaspal Singh

SIKH, Age 15

Calcutta lies low, flat and muggy on the Hooghly, a branch of the Ganges which forms a big delta in eastern India. The Hooghly is a lazy, yellow river that flows another one hundred and twenty miles beyond Calcutta, which lies flopped on either side, and empties into the Bay of Bengal. Calcutta is the largest city in India and the second largest in the British Commonwealth, with only London surpassing it in size and importance. It is Calcutta's pre-eminence in business and culture that has attracted people from all over India and even from other parts of the world. (The city has a large Chinese quarter.) Her cosmopolitan population is composed of enterprising businessmen from the West coast—Maharathis, Sindis, Rajastanis and Gujaratis—farm laborers from Uttar Pradesh, Bihar and Orissa, well-educated civil service professionals from the South, and Sikh entrepreneurs, mechanics and drivers from the Punjab. There are also West Bengalis from the outlying farms and about a million East Bengalis who came during the partition of 1947 when a section of India was lopped off and turned into East Pakistan. Jaspal Singh's father, a Sikh businessman, moved to Calcutta two years after Partition.

The Sikhs are one of the great minority groups of India. They grew out of an attempt by a Hindu holy man named Nanak, who wandered all over India preaching in both temples and mosques, to bring an end to the religious wars that were devastating both Hindus and Muslims in the fifteenth century. Nanak saw religion as a bond to unite people, not to separate them. What happened was that men of good will on both sides followed Nanak, and instead of healing the enmity between Hindu and Muslim, began a new religious movement—the Sikhs, or disciples. The Sikhs rejected both caste and racial pride, and rituals, pilgrimages, fasts and whatever kinds of religious observances might lead to conflict. Now there are Sikhs all over India. They are intelligent, aggressive, hard-working.

My father came to Calcutta in 1949 and we have been here since. I'm fifteen now. I have a brother seventeen, one fourteen and a sister eighteen. My father is an engineer with a company that makes small machinery parts. They're sub-contractors. My mother died three years ago. My father was brought up in England as a child and was there again during the war. We all speak English at home as a matter of course. A little bit of Punjabi and Bengali, but English is our home language. Hindi is being pushed by the central government [in New Delhi] as the Indian tongue, but it is not practical. English is. Hindi can't develop, it is not flexible enough. English develops and changes constantly. It's the one language in India that everyone understands. The South doesn't want Hindi, they prefer English. English should be the national language.

We have a lot of problems, but they can be solved. Take food, for example. There's enough food for everyone but it's not properly distributed. India is a good country, a great country, but there are so many problems, unnecessary, I think. Half of our food goes to waste. If I were Prime Minister [I had put the question to him] I would get the food properly distributed so that everyone could eat. I think the poor should get free rations. Family planning should be encouraged. The poor should have a chance at being educated. All many of them need is a chance to show themselves, to prove that they are as intelligent and as hard-working as anyone else and can get a job and do it properly.

We have a lot of corruption here, bribery of officials and companies getting jobs illegally. It could be stopped to a certain extent but not completely—there is always human nature to contend with.

I'm not interested in politics myself—they're too confusing, especially Indian politics (no one can follow them)—but politics in general. The war in Vietnam is not my interest. I can see both points of view. There's been practically no news about it in India, and, frankly, I'm not sure I can tell you the issues. I've followed the student riots abroad in *The New Statesmen*. I think the French and American students have been going too far, though to a certain extent they may be right. They need some freedom. They're checked in whatever they do—but I think setting fires is too much. The situation is different here in Calcutta. Bengali students are far rowdier than others. But you know, what makes Indian students demonstrate is something else. They object to the difficulty of the examinations. That's what sets them off. I think they should have studied harder. There were some riots in Bombay but again it was rowdiness. But personally, I don't get involved in politics. Whenever I try to find out which party is better than another I can't. I may like one party but my uncle may like another so we cancel each other out.

I've got my studies to think about. I'm hoping to go to the Indian Institute of Technology in Kanpur to study engineering and then if I'm lucky, to M.I.T. I'll have a try for a scholarship. America is a very advanced country.

[I remark to him that an Indian I had met earlier had said there

would be a dozen Vietnams in India because of the increasing social tensions.] That's going too far. I don't think it will happen. We should start to rebuild society by giving new hope, new life to the persons who are not well off. We should begin with family planning, we should make sure the poor have some rights, that they have education. We should prove to them that they have a place in life.

We are what you might call an advanced family. We are open to social problems, to changing conditions. I would marry a Hindu or a foreigner. I believe in love marriages. If I had an arranged marriage it would be to a Hindu girl, but a love marriage, to a foreigner. I couldn't marry a Muslim. Muslims have a grudge against the Sikhs. It would be wrong for me. They always start trouble against the Sikhs, and the Sikhs being human, try to retaliate. You can't blame us. There is great enmity between Muslims and Sikhs. I wouldn't marry an eastern girl, no Chinese for example. But a westerner, yes.

My father had an arranged marriage. I'd prefer a love marriage but I think my family will arrange one for me, to keep me from marrying the wrong girl. Arranged marriages go too far—catch hold of a girl and catch hold of a boy and put them together. My older brother thinks arranged marriages are all right. My sister doesn't have much choice. She's a quiet kind of a girl, not a bossy type, but minds her own affairs. My mother was a great person, very lovely. One of the strange things about her was that she could understand English perfectly but couldn't speak it. After giving us a beating she would explain why we deserved it. That's the kind of a person she was. And the kind a wife should be. I remember once that I took ten rupees [a lot of money] from my grandmother and spent it all. My mother gave me quite a beating and said that I shouldn't have taken it, and if I had, I should have put it in the bank. Only my mother beat me, not my father.

[I ask him about horoscopes.] Horoscopes? Oh, yes, oh yes. But if a horoscope foretells something bad I refuse to believe it. If it's good, yes. Usually the prediction comes true. For example, one day my horoscope said, "Today you will be quite popular." And do you know what happened? One of my teachers called me over and photographed me and put me in a magazine. Since then I've believed in them. I believe in the birth horoscope. [When an Indian child is born the parents have its horoscope cast immediately.] Mine says that I will get a degree at M.I.T. It says that I will have a beautiful wife and that I will live to a good old age, that I'll be rich, that I'll have a short temper (which I have) and that I'll have four or five children. Sometimes I have dreams where I come out as a hero. Superman stuff, like flying about, doing the impossible—becoming an invisible man and committing robberies. Everyone is in danger and I am a hero.

[Who are you?] A boy. A boy. An intelligent boy.

Ranjana Paul and Renana Jhabvala

STUDENTS, *Age 16*

anjana Paul and Renana Jhabvala are close friends. They live near each other and go to the same school. Both are sixteen. Ranjana's father is in the Indian diplomatic corps, Renana's father is an Indian architect, her mother, R. Prawer Jhabvala, writes short stories and novels, some of which have been turned into movies; she is originally a Polish Jew who escaped Hitler and grew up in England.

The Pauls and the Jhabvalas live in old Delhi, which was once the Mughal capital and now plays a secondary role to New Delhi, the center of Indian political and administrative life. Their homes are located in a pleasant, spacious area which resembles an English countryside, with a quiet road flanked by big leafy trees and houses with ample lawns and well-tended gardens. Walls and fences protect the houses from the occasional traffic on the road.

Mrs. Jhabvala says to me about the girls, "They're typical teenagers. I can't get a word out of them. I don't think you'll have any luck." The conversation alternates between the two girls. Renana begins by describing the school curriculum. I feel overwhelmed by the weight of what the modern upperclass Indian student must learn.

[Renana] This is what we have in school. We're now reading a simplified version of *Great Expectations*. Also short stories like P. G. Wodehouse, Rabindrath Tagore, Maugham, Galsworthy, Indian folk tales and so on. A book of simple poems: some Indians, Wordsworth, Shakespeare, Tagore, Cowper. Then, Pioneers of the Modern World: Bismarck, Tagore, Madame Curie, Andrew Carnegie, Lister, Ross, Marconi, Faraday. Grammar: we write essays—"My thoughts on the last day of school," "Describe a railway station," "What are your emotions." Our teacher is Mrs. Richards. Most of the teachers are Indian Christians.

Then we have mats [mathematics]—algebra, arithmetic, geometry (practical and theoretical), trigonometry, calculus, and statistics. Physics—mechanics, heat, light, sound, electrostatics and current electricity and magnetism. Modern physics and very elementary atomic physics. Chemistry—elementary organic and inorganic gases. Extracts and uses of metals. We had Hindi in the early grades. Instruction is now in English.

[Ranjana] We go to St. Mary's school. We're in the high secondary. That's the eleventh year, the last. I'd like to be a doctor. I see so much suffering among the people. They're very poor. My grandfather was a doctor. I was in his house once—I was four or five—and went with him to see a child in the neighborhood. The family was quite poor. It was January and they had no clothes [the Delhi area is extremely cold in the winter months]. That was when I decided to become a doctor. My sister—she'll be eighteen in a few months—was going to be a doctor, too, but now she is marrying a rich boy. She wasn't forced to, just asked. The boy is twenty-three.

He is the owner of a steel rolling mill. [*He* owns the mill?] Yes, he's the owner. The family bought the mill when it wasn't producing and put the boy in charge. He built it up and now it supplies most of the steel in Uttar Pradesh.

[The sister is marrying a boy of the same caste. The Pauls are Vaishya, which is the third of the four major groups. Ranjana continues.] We don't believe in caste. Caste is very superficial. You might find a Sudra [the fourth caste, which is considered a great step below the first three] who is well-educated and a Brahmin who is not. A man should be judged by his deeds, not his birth. My parents feel the same way. Caste has already disappeared in many places. I myself would marry a man of another caste. And I wouldn't marry to please my parents.

Every girl dreams she'll marry a handsome husband. I'd like my husband to be a doctor. I hope he'll be handsome, but that is not important. In India we generally have arranged marriages. I would prefer one. I think it's always better because your parents see it clearer. If I fall in love, all right. Otherwise it will be arranged. I think an arranged marriage can be happy.

[Renana] I don't approve of arranged marriages at all. They get to be too arranged—everything planned out for you by everyone else. I don't see why that should be. Marriage is such an important thing. I don't know what kind of man I would want to marry—it's too early at my age for me to tell. Even if I married I would have a job.

[Ranjana] When I was three and a half we went to Moscow. My father is in the Ministry of External Affairs. We flew via London and spent fifteen days there. London was rainy: it had dark and cloudy streets. I remember Selfridges—a very nice store. We spent two and a half years in Moscow. People were very nice to us and we had a good apartment. I could speak Russian but now I've forgotten it. I've been to Kashmir, Rajastan and Bombay.

[Renana] I've been in England twice. The first time was when I was six. I don't remember that trip at all. Then I went again when I was eight. I was alone on the plane. My grandmother met me. I was frightened traveling alone but I was also proud of myself. We stayed in a suburb of London. I came back alone too.

[Ranjana] I don't go to the movies often. I saw *My Fair Lady* recently. It's a very nice movie. I've seen only half a dozen western movies—usually I go to Hindi films. I like the Beatles—some of their numbers—but not all. I listen to the radio (we hear the eight o'clock news broadcasts). I like Hindi movie music but not classical. There's a singer named Kundan Lalsaikal who used to be an actor who is my favorite. He's got such a deep melodious voice!

[Renana] I read a lot—almost everything. I don't like Dickens. I read Maugham, Galsworthy, Wodehouse [part of the school's reading list]. I read *Gone with the Wind*. I seldom read magazines. I like science fiction very much.

[Ranjana] I read a lot of magazines—*Femina, Reader's Digest, Life, Woman and House, Sarite* (it's a Hindi magazine), *Eve's Weekly, Time, Science Reporter* and *Science Today* (they're both published in India), the *Hindustan Times* and the *Times of India*, both the daily and the Sunday editions. I read detective novels. I read *Gone with the Wind*, too.

[I ask about hippies, a popular topic. Renana speaks.] I don't approve of them at all. Mostly the dirt. The looseness. You see them walking around. They just look dirty. [I remark that the poor people in India look dirty too.] But they can't help that. I agree that people should rebel against things but it's the way they go about it. [Ranjana says her piece about hippies.] I don't think that more than ten percent of Americans are hippies. I don't think it is their personality that they would behave in this manner—they are being led forward by others. They leave their studies and all—they're just wasting their lives. If a person followed his studies he could help his country. All they want is money.

[What would Ranjana do if she had money?] Many times I thought that if I were a doctor, I would open a nice hospital. I could expand my business if I had a clinic, a nursing home, a clinic in a small town. Then I'd like a nice home in the country, open country, where you could go horseback riding. I'd open a school. I would invest, re-invest my money—in a school, a factory, in something or other.

[I put the Question and then ask about dreams.]

[Ranjana] A girl. A girl. An Indian. . . . My dream goes like this. Two days back I had a physics paper. In my dreams I was worried I had not done it.

[Renana on the same] Me. Well, I think there are two of me. Two of me. [Why?] When I say two of me, there's a "higher" me and a "lower" me. There's a higher me that watches me. I've always been there, always been watching. As I'm talking, I'm watching myself. I don't talk to myself, though at night I do. I go over what I've been doing. Sometimes we laugh at me. "I" am all that I would like to be. "I" am for one very intelligent. (I don't mean I, I mean me.) "I" am always calm, never get excited. "I" am self-assured.

I only have dreams about exams nowadays. When I have nightmares I am trying to solve things. I go round and round in circles. [A dream] Just during the exam, I finished my mats paper and brought it home and found I hadn't done anything. I don't know if I became an old man or if the old man was there—he was going to do my paper for me and I said no and pulled off his beard and that was all. I don't remember who he was, but he was somebody.

[Renana on India] I'm not very sure about the future. I sort of feel that India is degenerating more and more. If anyone wished to colonize it now, it would be very easy. I don't mean anyone in particular. It would be easy to overthrow—there's so much disagreement. [What should be done?] For one thing, prevent the brain drain. For another, stop the quarrels between the parties. There's a lot of dishonesty. For example, in the exams everybody cheats. It should be stopped in school. You take a liberal attitude in school. Then it goes on. There is no real penalty for cheating. Nobody believes it's serious. [*Eve's Weekly,* a popular woman's magazine, in an article on teenagers in a special issue devoted to

them, reports: "Taking a bribe is not considered a great sin—only 'he shouldn't be caught.'" No boys condemned taking bribes, though a few girls did.]

I visited the Jhabvalas a number of times. They are a pleasant, witty, intelligent family. One night Mr. Jhabvala and I were sitting in the garden. He was talking about dating and marriage.

"Dating is always in groups. Arranged marriages, love marriages—both have the same chance of success or failure. Girls won't go out alone with a boy anyway. They can't walk in the park, can't go to the movies, can't hold hands. If the girl is willing to go out alone with a boy, then everyone thinks she comes from a 'bad' family and the boy doesn't want to marry into it. And the caste system is very strong no matter what anyone tells you. Arranged marriages preserve caste." Mrs. Jhabvala mentioned an article the same day in the *Hindustan Times* about untouchables. The report showed that prejudice against untouchables is almost total. To a foreigner, untouchables look the same as other Indians, and he cannot tell them from people of higher castes; an increasing number of untouchables get education and jobs and live on the same economic level as caste Indians. But to a Hindu, they are still untouchable. Mrs. Jhabvala was quite upset over the condition of the untouchables.

Mr. Jhabvala went on to mention the marriage advertisements which are a common feature of the Sunday newspapers. Foreigners, as I know from my own reaction, have a morbid interest in them. They advertise marriageable young people like any other commodity, a car, a toaster, a radio, clothing, a dentifrice, touting the good qualities and glossing over the poor ones, like weak eyes or shortness or dark skin. A standard adjective for a girl is "homely." "Do you know what homely means?" asked Mr. Jhabvala. "Homemaker," I said. "No, yes, everything. How to get along on four hundred a month. If the man is rich, how to arrange things on the mantle. How to entertain. And she wears her hair piled on top."

A GROUP OF UNTOUCHABLES. THE BOY AND WOMAN
SHOW THE EFFECTS OF POOR NUTRITION.

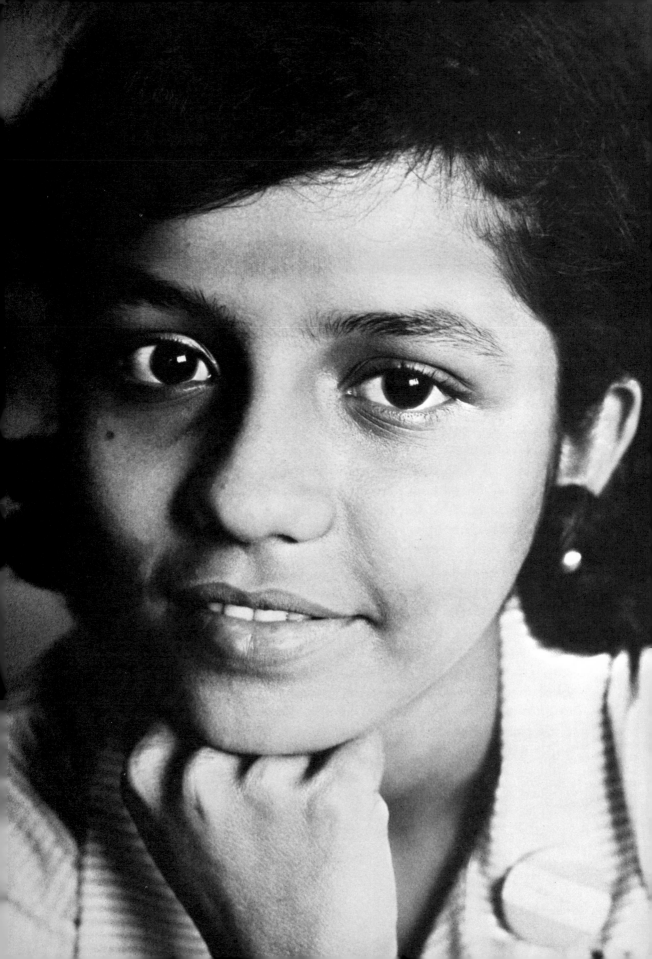

Juliana D'Silva

ANGLO-INDIAN, Age 15

A very small person, only four foot nine. But very intelligent, creative, the most unusual young Indian I spoke to. And, perhaps rather unhappy. Juliana D'Silva is an Anglo-Indian, a very special group of the many that form India. India has always had a special facility for absorbing new groups and turning them into a part of herself, an all-encompassing, all-loving mother with infinite compassion who can also be a mother who never takes to certain of her children. When the Europeans, the Portuguese, Dutch, French and British arrived in India, the intermingling and marriages of their soldiers, adventurers, businessmen and clerks with Indian women produced colonies of half-castes. In the West and South the Portuguese baptized some, married a few and left behind the varied Indians erroneously grouped together as Goans. In Calcutta and a few other cities the British produced the Anglo-Indians, a minority who have maintained a special identity despite many vicissitudes. Accepted by the British only to the extent of their usefulness as clerks and as a bridge to Indians, and rejected by orthodox Hindus and Muslims, they became in effect a separate nation within India. Their thinking was English, their way of life a mixture of English and Indian. Many went into civil service, business, the railways and a few into the Army. Some were highly successful and made fortunes. They had a closed community, usually marrying among themselves, wearing western clothes and bearing a nostalgia for a land they would never see. Independence was a blow to them.

Juliana D'Silva's great-grandfather was Scottish. She has been brought up in the Anglo-Indian community in Calcutta, speaking English at home and attending a western mission school run by the Assembly of God Church, an American evangelistic group. Juliana is now fifteen and is in her next-to-last year at school, the equivalent of America's second year of high school.

I lost my father. He isn't dead. He left when I was a baby. Mum was alone with four girls. A lady brought her to the Assembly of God Church. We used to be R.C.'s. Mum gets spiritual guidance here. Now I prefer the A.G.C. I enjoy the services. I've written a play for the school. It's based on the New Testament story of the centurion and the servant. A teacher directed it.

I've been writing seriously for several years. I need some money to go to college—I'll have to work somewhere first, so now I am doing magazine and newspaper articles. I've written for *The Mirror,* the *Hindustan Standard, Amrita Bazar,* papers like that. They are articles on different subjects: "Time the Inexorable Factor"; "Why Trees are My First Love"; "Great White Beautiful Worderful World"—I describe a sunset; "The Ethereal World of the Child"; "Beast of Burden." I usually get paid about twenty-five or thirty rupees, but a few papers don't pay at all. But it's good

to be published. Mr. Sassoon [a teacher] helps me. I write a covering letter and my sister types the manuscripts.

My Mum is short too. We're all short except my married sister who is sort of medium and would like to go to Australia with her husband and my second sister who is tall. We come out about half and half, don't we? My Mum is very cheerful and hardworking, not like me. She runs a boarding house on Sandal Street.

I don't like housework. I read a lot—murder, romance, history, poetry, anything I can lay my hands on. I'd like to go to the movies but the Church doesn't allow us. But we do hear the radio, the classical musical program. I mean western classical, like Beethoven. I don't like Indian music. It has a funny effect on me. I enjoy it and so on, but I prefer western. I love to play musical instruments —we have a piano—but I don't know much about them. I paint when I get a chance. I'm busy all the time. I have some pen pals, and I go swimming and cycling. We have a dog and two parrots; we had a squirrel but he died. School takes up a lot of time. We get Bengali and Hindi all through school—I get them mixed up: both sound the same. English, mathematics, algebra, geography, earth science, Indian and world history, religion—we're reading St. John now.

I want to become a traveling journalist ["Like you," she says to me]. I've always wanted to see the world. Then I'll settle down. [Anglo-Indians believe in love marriages. What kind of a man would she like to marry? She is shy about the question.] The ideal man? He has to be masterful. I've got a very bad temper, you know, so he'll have to put up with my tantrums. I haven't met him yet. I want to marry someone from the West if I ever get married. If I don't meet the ideal man I might be an old maid. My ideal man will have to be rich.

My palm says that I'll be rich, very successful and have a long life. I believe in palm reading but not horoscopes. My palm also says that I'll have many husbands.

[The Question] Juliana. Myself. My mother's daughter. [Why

these answers?] That's my name, Juliana. I suppose I have an Indian character. I'm not her son.

I dream about people. Mostly events that happened during the day. They get mixed up in my dreams at night. They don't take a definite shape. Once I dreamed a poem. It was a holy poem. I wrote it down but I lost it.

When Juliana was a child several people stated that she was a genius. Mr. Sassoon, the teacher who helps her place her articles, tells me that her father walked out about eleven or twelve years ago. "All the girls are very negative. You have to force them to work. Juliana is very humble about herself. I'm surprised that she talked so much. The father is still in Calcutta. He's said to be unemployed and unemployable. When *The Catholic Herald* [a local paper] did something on Juliana he was furious."

I had asked both Juliana and Mr. Sassoon about the name D'Silva. Both emphasized that it was not Portuguese as it seems but "some kind of European name." Among Mother India's unwanted children, if you cannot be British, at least you can be European and not Portuguese.

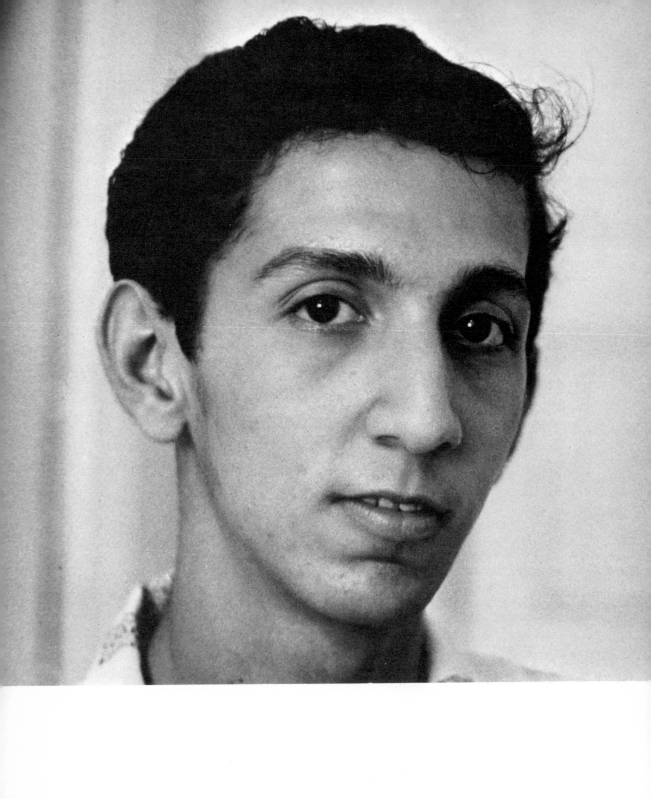

Sohail Madni

MUSLIM OFFICE WORKER, Age 18

Sohail Madni is an eighteen-year-old office worker who has recently graduated from high school and is now employed in a Bombay office as an apprentice in a company that manufactures machines, batteries, spark plugs, motor parts and refrigerators. He is training to be a secretary. His family, who are Muslim, emigrated from Kutch, a poor, arid area in Northwest India which was split during Partition in 1947 and has since been the scene of minor armed clashes between India and Pakistan.

There are some sixty million Muslims in India, roughly ten or eleven percent of the total population. They form the third largest Muslim community in the world after Pakistan and Indonesia; there are more Muslims in India than in all the Arab nations of the Middle East and

North Africa. Hindus and Muslims have had communal clashes for many decades. It was this tension—religious, social and economic—which helped bring about the creation of Pakistan as a separate Muslim nation out of two sections of India. In a recent four-year period, between 1964 and 1968, local rioting against Muslims resulted in the deaths of 1250 Muslims and 250 Hindus. This is four times the number of casualties in similar rioting during the previous fourteen years. Both Hindus and Muslims in India will say, "We can get along very well without these disturbances, if only the other fellow will mind his own business and respect other peoples' rights."

There is no doubt that Muslims suffer wide discrimination as a group. Only two percent of the top government officials are Muslim, and only one half of one percent of the clerks and messengers. One reason for these low figures is that many Muslims, whether justified or not, fear discrimination and will not attempt to enter certain categories of employment. The result is that Muslims tend to become more and more withdrawn into their own communities, living and working together, and incurring charges from Hindus of wanting to be a separatist nation within India. A few well-to-do Muslims emigrate to Pakistan or to England (where they are still subject to discrimination as "Pakis" and "little brown brothers"). But mass migration is impossible for the majority of Muslims. They are too poor to pull up stakes and go to Pakistan, which has one hundred and twenty million people of its own and is even poorer than India.

> I'm working only part time. I would like to go to college to study arts and sciences—by that I mean social sciences as opposed to true science subjects. Someday I hope to get a job in Voltas [a large engineering company]. I've got a good job. I'm learning everything. I've been promoted twice since I began and now I'm learning the telephone switchboard.
>
> There are a lot of changes taking place today. We're beginning to feel the generation gap, in Bombay, anyway. I believe that parents are very strict with their children. Why? They want their chil-

dren to be something in life, to go beyond their own position. They want to discipline you so you don't waste your potential. I think that's right. In the long run you benefit. Most often parents are right. I have complete trust in my father. He is a law-abiding citizen.

I owe a responsibility to my parents. There is no real tension between me and them. I'm the oldest child—I have two brothers and two sisters, all younger—I must help them. As the oldest child I must assume a lot. They allow me to go out but very seldom alone with girls. Sometimes I go out in groups. In the middle teens dating is all right, but when you're older you must concentrate on the future. It's one or the other. You can't date if you are working. Do western children have more freedom? [I said Yes.] I'm not jealous.

We are Suni Muslims. I'm very religious but since I've been working I have no time to go to the mosque on Fridays. I fast during Ramadan [a period of prayer and fasting roughly comparable to Lent] but not strictly. I don't have time to follow the Muslim prayers during the day. We should pray five times. I read the Koran in Arabic. I'd like to make a pilgrimage to Mecca. A person must go at least once in his life. If you are well off in life, you must go. God doesn't tell us to do it—it's the individual's own desire.

There is no caste system among us as there is among the Hindus, but we consider ourselves superior to the Kodjais [another Muslim group]. They have a lot of money but no education or culture. They're very lewd-speaking people, very uncouth. Intermarriage with other religions is allowed and takes place, but me, I wouldn't marry anyone who is not a Muslim. I wouldn't marry an African— I discriminate in that. A Christian, perhaps, if she is attractive. But our marriages are arranged. Girls are not allowed to choose their marriage partners. They can date after their parents have arranged the marriage, after their parents have consented. My main objective is to marry a Muslim. I have a great feeling of my own religion. One must stay true to his own background.

The kind of girl I'd like must be sociable and get along with her parents. I wouldn't want family quarrels after marriage. But I wouldn't accept my family's choice, though. It's too big a risk. I'd want something to say. I don't have a girl now. I won't marry until I'm twenty-eight or so. Children [an embarrassed laugh]—just a couple. A woman should be a good citizen. She has to look after the house. She must pray twice a day. An unmarried woman can work, but when she marries her main place is in the home. I wouldn't encourage a wife to work.

We are in a kind of a box here, being Muslims in a Hindu nation. I have mixed feelings. Sometimes I would like to emigrate—I don't know where to. Bombay is a very cosmopolitan city. I feel at home here, but as far as the nation goes, I have no feeling for it. My father plans on emigrating to Pakistan—he is very much inclined towards Pakistan, but it's not the place for us. In Pakistan life is just a series of clubs. Here you can go to the beach and there are a lot of other things to do. I know about Karachi [the capital of West Pakistan] only from hearsay. Emigration is the only way to come up. I'd go to Pakistan first, if I had decided to emigrate, then to Canada or England or the States. Or, for a few years only, to Russia or Italy. But not to China.

[What do you think of President Zakir Husain? He is a Muslim.] Oh, Husain, he's just a dummy, a figurehead. He doesn't fool me. We suspect him very much.

The Hindus have treated the Muslims very badly in the past five years. We as a family have not experienced prejudice but the Hindus in our apartment house seem prejudicial. Muslims have trouble in getting ahead in business and government unless they are very brilliant. So many Muslims are not being hired. We don't stand a chance here.

If there is a real war between India and Pakistan [there have been many clashes] China will step in. But they're both beggars, India and Pakistan, they won't fight. But if there were a war, we'd be massacred, not so much in Bombay but in the other cities.

He has some small conflicts with his father. They have fights over pocket money. His father doesn't want him to drive fast cars. "But I would reason with him if I ever wanted to get a car." He can't recall dreams—he couldn't grasp the idea of a subconscious mind and it had to be explained to him. "I'm too involved at work to dream. None for the last few days. I've been sleeping like a log. Before that I dreamed about my examinations. You get the creeps afterward about whether you passed or failed. But I never put any significance in dreams." The Question: "I'm a teenager," he says after thinking. "A working person." He can't answer a third time and remarks about his first answer that when you meet a person you explain who you are. Sohail is tall and gangly, straightforward and intelligent. The family is moderately well-off. He says his uncles are "intellectuals," meaning well-educated. The family has a sweeper girl. They eat breakfast at home, but lunch and dinner at the grandmother's home, a loose kind of joint family. On Thursdays and Fridays some cousins join them for meals. I ask him what great men he admires. He names Eisenhower, Churchill and Kennedy. So much for India. And what about great women? He can't think of any and is embarrassed.

Later in the day the announcement was made that President Husain had died that morning. India mourned, offices were closed, world leaders paid tributes, and India replaced him with a Hindu.

Sharoukh
E. Bharucha

PARSI, Age 15

Sharoukh E. Bharucha and Hoshi Dorab Beboo are Parsis. Both are fifteen. Hoshi is smaller, quieter and less tense and fades into the background as we talk in a side room in their school. Sharoukh is so taut he seems to be about to snap. Life is serious for him, and he knows that he is representing all Parsis to me. The headmaster has given him a good talking to before we meet. I ask Sharoukh about some Parsis I have visited. He doesn't know them, but I can see a cloud passing over his face: should he say he does to be polite? But then that would not be honest. An ordinary Indian might have said yes, or at least fudged the question, I think, merely to be friendly and keep the conversation going.

The Parsis have an undeservedly notorious reputation because they follow the god Mazda and his prophet Zoroaster and worship in fire temples, and worst of all, dispose of their dead in Towers of Silence, where they are consumed by vultures. The vultures drop pieces of arms and legs on the surrounding buildings. Mark Twain, who visited Bombay a century ago, was alternately fascinated, horrified and scandalized, a typical American reaction. He saw more than most people ever have, except the Parsi priests, and wrote pages about it. But the Tower of Silence is a gruesome method of disposing of the dead, and younger Parsis today object to the custom and are demanding that the dead be cremated in the Hindu manner. The Parsi community is split, as it has been many times in the past over various issues, and it is also dwindling. It is one which has shown great vitality and longevity. Some of the great industrialists are Parsi, as are many of the doctors, lawyers, architects, and philanthropists, but at the same time centuries of inbreeding have sapped some of the life force. There are many childless marriages, and even so, only fifty percent of Parsis marry. The birth rate is twelve per thousand, compared to the all-India rate of forty-five per thousand. The world population of Parsis is small—some one hundred thousand or a few more in India, primarily in and around Bombay, twenty to thirty thousand in Iran, where they originated, about sixty-five hundred in Pakistan, and a few thousand in Canada, America and the rest of the world.

The Parsis are Zoroastrians, the fire people who once ruled ancient Persia. Theirs was the basic religion, one which was supreme and powerful and at that time an equal to any other in influence and subtlety. It was the Zoroastrians, the Persians, who dominated the Middle East, threatened Greece and Egypt and fought Byzantium to a standstill. Then, after the country had been weakened by dissension and wars, the Arabs invaded Persia, bringing not only a new rule but a new religion and culture, which was quickly adopted by the mass of the Persian people. The Zoroastrians fled, some to China, where they died out, and others to the west coast of India, where they were given sanctuary on the condition that they would not try to make converts. The emphasis on this prohibition has shifted, so that today the Parsis will not accept a convert even if one should apply. The Parsis settled down

—the exact date is not known but it was roughly in the seventh century A.D.—and for years were a quiet, hard-working agricultural community, minding their own business and hardly leaving a mark on India. Much of what happened during this early period is unknown, except that they did build fire temples and Towers of Silence. Apparently they had not brought religious books with them, so they performed their ceremonies by memory. During the late fourteenth century there was persecution of Zoroastrian communities that had remained in Persia and some of them fled to India, bringing liturgical and religious books. Over the next three hundred years Parsi priests and scholars visited Persia on numerous occasions to study the correct doctrines and practices and re-vitalized the Indian communities. The Parsis were also becoming prosperous, not only in agriculture but in weaving, ship-building, coastal trade, toddy-tapping and various crafts and businesses. The one area denied them for religious reasons was black-smithing and anything associated with a profane use of fire, since fire is a sacred element. In 1700 Parsi carpenters were hired to build ships for the British at a trading post called Surat. This was the beginning of a very large ship-building industry, which made several fortunes for the Parsis and enabled them to spread into other businesses. When the British moved from Surat to Bombay further South and made that city their headquarters in western India, the Parsis followed. Their prosperity, and their intellectual, cultural and philanthropical pre-eminence stems from this close association with the British. They were the first Indians to cross the ocean (travel upon water was, and is, prohibited to strict Hindus), the first community in India to educate its women, the first to sponsor hospitals and social services. Since the Europeans touched the shores of India, the Parsis have been useful to them as middlemen in trading and banking and in dealing with the various Indian states and rulers. Today the Parsis represent power far beyond their numbers. Some of the big industrialists and businessmen are Parsis, who are very liberal in charitable enterprises, and in developing cultural and intellectual projects, bestowing grants from foundations on an American scale. They are prim, proper, intelligent, hardworking, conscientious. But they also seem, some of them, to be on the edge of their nerve.

They may laugh, but, after seeing some Parsi social events, my personal impression is that I have never seen a jolly Parsi.

It is a muggy spring morning when I visit the Dadar Parsi Youths Assembly High School, in the Mancherji Joshi Colony, a Parsi community in Bombay. The principal, Mr. M. D. Hodiwalla, an intense small man, who looks not the least bit "Indian" but more like a true Persian, brings out Sharoukh and Hoshi. He tells me they are the brightest boys in the school and leaders in their class. My first, unspoken impression is that these are the most uptight kids I've met in years. They are tense, on the edges of their seats, nervous about making a bad impression on me, and speak as if every word has to be measured in the light of eternity. I appreciate their position. I am a stranger, and no one knows quite what I want or what the outcome will be. After we have met, Mr. Hodiwalla asks the entire school to stand on the street (it's called Firdoshi Road, after an old Persian poet) so I can talk to them. There is some shoving and pushing, so Mr. Hodiwalla and the teachers wack a few heads and blow their whistles and shout and in a few moments the students stand respectfully still. I go upstairs to a balcony to take a photograph of the entire school, not previously having seen so many Parsis at once. Then Mr. Hodiwalla tells the students, who are still standing in the street, that I am going to talk to them. "Look!" he says to the school, "Here is this fine gentleman who has come all the way from America just to see you." I expect him to add "you ungrateful wretches." But he says, "Now let me hear you cheer." They give three cheers and I applaud. I say a few words in American about what an honor it is to see so many fine young Parsi gentlemen and how I have two teenage sons who would have loved to meet them and how it is all one world. No one understands my accent, but I am having trouble with theirs, too. We all thank each other and the school disperses.

> My father is resident assistant in the CIBA Research Centre. He is a chemist. I'd like to be a doctor, perhaps even a surgeon. Many Parsis are doctors, you know. I was born in Bombay. We live here, a few miles from the school. I come down by bus: we have to be

here at 8:45 and we end at four. It's a full schedule: mats [mathematics], English, Hindi, French, Gujarati, science—physics and chemistry—, history and geography. The next year Gujarati (that's our home language anyhow) and history will be dropped and will be replaced by social studies and special geography.

We are interested in the modern world. Parsis have been very much involved in building a new India, in business and medicine and architecture and industry. We like to know what is going on. [What about China?] China? That is our most dreaded enemy. The world situation is dangerous. America, Russia, China—they have those nuclear weapons which can turn the world into powder. I'm afraid of world war between the nuclear nations. India must plunge in. [But he is not sure on which side.] I'm interested in the space program. America's achievement is impressive. The Russians are very secretive. India is not able to join in. We have no manpower and no good research.

There is so much chaos and evil. I see those foreign hippies. They're nomads. No taste, no good morals. All they do is dance about. I like the Beatles—they came to India—but I fear they might have a bad influence on our way of life. I like Indian movies but not western. Indian movies show our culture, our heritage. Our morality [which is what?]. The clothes, the manners. We wear western clothes at school but during the religious ceremonies we wear Indian clothes. [On the wall is a badly executed but interesting drawing.] Do you see what this represents: it is our Parsi symbol. Good words, good thoughts, good deeds. These are the three main pillars of our religion. We should lead a righteous life on earth. Bad thoughts, bad words, bad deeds will keep us from Heaven. We must lead a good life in order to go to Heaven. That is the Parsi teaching.

The next day we meet after school has ended. Miss Lal is with me. I think I have shown her more of India than she ever suspected existed. On the other hand, she reads more American magazines than I do and knows more about my country. We seem to come out even. Hoshi and

Sharoukh show us through the community. It is large and well-tended, with very spacious houses on wide streets. In the center is a big maidan or field, where some Parsi boys are playing cricket. The scene is very English, the boys in short gray pants and white shirts. Their faces are washed and their hair neatly trimmed and their shoes are shined. A few elderly men pass by, in *dhotis* (the male version of the sari, worn in sweeping folds), black jackets and little black hats and carrying umbrellas against the sun. Younger Parsi men wear western business suits and have to have air-conditioned offices in order to bear the heat their clothes create.

I ask Hoshi and Sharoukh if I can see the local fire temple (there are five in Bombay). I'd like to get inside, something that is forbidden to foreigners, but there is always the chance that the rules might be waived. The boys bring me to the gate. It is open, but both of them stand before it as if they were defending it. Sharoukh looks particularly anxious and I decide it is best not to press the point. What happens inside a Parsi fire temple is known but the Parsis don't talk about it. What Sharoukh does tell me is that "if you want, you can pray every day, but it is expensive." The layman does not pray himself, but asks a priest to do so. A voluntary offering to the priest is necessary. I'd like to know what goes on in the Tower of Silence too, but I don't press Sharoukh. He has been very good for the past two days and there is no point in making him any more nervous. However, he says he has received the thread. "We have the thread ceremony between the ages of seven and nine. It is an initiation when we receive the *kusti,* the thread, and the *sadre,* the white shirt." Except while bathing a Zoroastrian must always wear the sacred thread and shirt, which are the signs of his membership in the Parsi community. The thread is untied and tied on the following occasions, according to a Parsi manual given me later: "immediately after leaving bed in the morning; every time after answering a call of nature; before saying prayers; at the time of bathing; before meals." It adds: "The *Datastani Denik* says that, from times immemorial, men turn towards the light at the time of performing the *kusti* ceremony as is connected with a form of prayer."

While the knot is being retied, there is a sequence of four thoughts on the Absolute to be followed. Many ceremonies are done in the presence of a fire. There is one ceremony that I will mention merely for its curiosity value. I am intrigued by things like this. It is the *bareshnum,* a ritual of purification which is performed in the presence of a "four-eyed" dog. The person being purified touches the left ear of the dog with his left hand. The dog's four eyes are his natural eyes and two spots under them. The four eyes are said to double the efficacy of his gaze. The four-eyed dog is also employed in the funeral rite, when he is led into the presence of the corpse. This custom is called *sagdid* or "dog sight." The dog is supposed to sense or smell if the person might still be alive. His eyes are believed to have a magnetic power. The dog is present also on account of his loyalty to man. A four-eyed dog obviously has a busy life. We might fruitfully employ them here in America to prevent the excesses of our morticians, who will embalm first and question later.

The emergence of the Parsis as a powerful and creative force in India after nearly ten centuries of bare existence is a phenomenon that has intrigued many people. Once they developed their contacts with the western nations that invaded India, they became the most modern, adventurous and dynamic group in all India. This sudden vitality was cited by an American geographer, Ellsworth Huntington of Yale, in a study of the effect of race and environment on civilization. He said the Parsis were a community tried but fortified by natural selection which allows only the fittest to survive. But today, with all their power, wealth, and altruism, they seem to be wavering.

Kakoo

STUDENT REBEL, *Age 18*

K akoo (his real name is Amitabh Adhar) was reading the forms for emigrating to Switzerland when I met him. I had been told that he was a true student rebel, and he tried to live up to his reputation, quoting Mao and Che Guevara and saying India should be blown up—there was no other solution. After several days with him I decided that the rebellion was all on the surface. Basically he is a very traditional young man and spoiled. He is eighteen, tall, attractive and quite vocal. His father is well-to-do (they have three automobiles), and owns an extensive amount of real estate. The family has a nice single-level house in the heart of New Delhi, near the famous Connaught Circus, the area from which all other streets radiate. Kakoo said they were about to buy their own television set—most are communally owned by villages; the standard set costs $250, a year's income for an average family.

I can't stand India, I've got to get out. There are thirty or forty thousand unemployed graduate engineers. (It's the most expensive course to study.) But there's no future. If I go abroad I've got a chance. If I stay, I don't. The whole country is about to explode. Nothing is going properly. Take education, for example. In lower school the teachers were O.K. but not very well educated. We are taught a lot of lies. Whatever history we were taught in school was all rot. The facts were wrong. The teacher didn't have the latest information. Take the Emperor Akbar for instance. In school we were taught that Akbar had developed a new religion. It wasn't a new religion, it was a synthesis. Akbar took Hinduism, Islam and Buddhism and perhaps a touch of Christianity and made a very eclectic kind of worship. We are taught that this was a religious movement, but basically it was political. It wasn't at all spiritual.

Let me give you another example. In school we learned that Aurangzeb was a very orthodox Muslim and used to persecute Hindus and torture them—that he was a bad man. Now I can realize that he was not so orthodox. The school books say he used to demolish Hindu temples to hurt Hindu religious sensibilities. Now I know that his actions were political. After they had attacked the Mughal armies, the Hindus would hide in the temples, so naturally Aurangzeb attacked them. What the books don't say is that in times of peace Aurangzeb contributed to the temples.

The main problem for Indians today is not religion [New Delhi is the background for constant Hindu-Muslim conflicts]. It is how Indians can feed themselves. Unemployment, social security, caste, religion are secondary things. If I were asked to become a Muslim in order to get a good job, I wouldn't mind. All religions are equally irrelevant, but not equally good. The proscriptions against Hindus eating meat mean nothing. I've tried beef and I like it, but somehow it doesn't suit me. I get pimples. We eat eggs but otherwise we are completely vegetarian.

But I must leave India. I'd like to emigrate to Switzerland. We can get jobs abroad but not here. There's no security in India. We must change social conditions. We get so disgusted. Conditions will get worse. In the current framework you can never change society. Most people don't want to change it. Either they're too disgusted or they've given up hope. Or they're profiting by it.

There will be a revolution. Nobody can stop it. It will not be non-violent, but violent. Thoroughly bloody—because the people have become so bitter. A violent revolution, you see, because of conditions. My poor friends make remarks about what is coming. On the one hand people are scared of what will happen, but revolution is the only alternative. Even the rich are ready for the revolution. It will be bloody: the rich will leave their properties in order to save their lives. Peaceful change will not work now. Parliamentary means are not enough. I don't know exactly when events will break, but it will be whenever there are enough strikes to lead to full scale upheaval. I'd say in ten or fifteen years, because there are people working for it. They are a small number, but they are dedicated.

How will it affect us? I don't know. My father is a businessman. He speculates in land. He was once manager of the All India Spinners Association and a strong Gandhiite. We come from Kashmir. My father had never eaten with a knife and fork until he met some westerners in Delhi.

[I ask him what he thinks about Mrs. Gandhi's government.] I don't think about it. Everyone is corrupt. We are patient, that is why we are suffering, but we are violent too. How can a peon [an office messenger] feed eight or ten children on 150 rupees a month? No wonder they take bribes. But corruption starts at the top. I personally think that if all the cabinet ministers were placed in a row and shot that would stop corruption. Unless you change the whole society nothing will change. Bribery and corruption will exist as long as there are no violent changes.

I am leading a comfortable life, but . . . I am impressed with Communism. I am not a Communist however. They say that

under Communism there is no freedom of speech, but I think it is the best system for India. Seventy-five families control the government and all the resources; in Pakistan it is seven.

[He smiles; he has a kind of cat-like grin when he is pleased.] I'll tell you about Che. He was a romantic revolutionary. But he didn't have sound theory. He was a brave man, no doubt about that. I've read his *Diary*—it's, what shall I say, it's OK, it's not a masterpiece. But OK, yes. I admire him because in places he admits his failures. He led a tough sort of life in the jungles. I don't think he should have gone to Bolivia. The family that got him shot —well, he shouldn't have tried to bribe them. You have to influence their way of thinking.

Revolution is something that no outsider can initiate. The local people have to take the initiative. I think Che has become very popular. In India people are trying to copy him—beards, cigars, that kind of thing. [I never saw any of these Che types.] I heard that in Europe instead of saying good morning, people say Che! Indian youth has been influenced a lot by the Chinese, especially by Mao. Mao says that only the local people can fight. No outsider can. The revolution can't be exported. It has to be indigenous. Che was shot because he was a fool. But I think we need such brave people here to start a revolution. The same can happen in India.

[I ask him about Indian marriage customs—virtually all marriages are arranged by the parents.] Personally I think they're all rot. Stupid customs! You go along with them because people say you shouldn't hurt the feelings of your elders. [His sister, who is twenty, has chosen her own boyfriend. He is an amateur pilot. His older brother was killed in a plane crash, yet the mother allows the younger son to fly anyway. Why doesn't she forbid it, I ask.] It's God's will if he gets killed or lives. I'm not interested in sports myself. I've played everything, even used to lift weights. But I like the outdoor life. I like fast cars but since I am the only son I am not allowed to have a sports car. My parents give me a lot of "don'ts." I'm eighteen, I'm a major, but since we depend on them for our future, we have to listen to them. But the system we're in makes no

DWELLINGS OF THE POOR ON A STREET IN BOMBAY.

sense. They've spent thirty or forty thousand rupees on my education, and I'll get a job at 150. If that money had been put in a bank, I'd get 500 rupees in interest. I've got a chance of earning some money if I go abroad. Here servants get 150 rupees and food, a graduate engineer gets 150 and no food. A driver for a foreigner gets four or five hundred. [A rupee is worth about ten cents.]

Here's an example of what goes on. The teacher told the son of our driver that he needed tutoring. The driver couldn't afford it—he earns only 200 rupees and the teacher wanted eighty—so the son was flunked. Now the son has become a motor mechanic, has a wife and a son of his own and earns ninety rupees a month.

[*Another day.*]

I've had eleven years of secondary education—in Hindi—and now I'm in my second year at Hindu College in New Delhi University. It's English medium. I'm confused between the languages. I can't think properly in one or the other. I have one more year for my B.A., and then two years at the University for my M.A.

[I ask a few questions to see what he knows of the world.] Your space program is doing very well. I'm not against it—it's a good thing to explore space, but it's a very big expenditure of money. If America cut down on arms, they could spend it on space. With all those enormous resources on hand they could help other countries. Educate the poor. People will think of what is good and what is bad and help themselves. Then there won't be any need of Communism. Everything is at America's disposal. There's American influence everywhere. In India, one out of three rupees is owned by America. [This is the result of the U.S. foreign aid program. Payment is set aside for America but not collected.] Whatever America gives us goes to the wrong people. The ministers get the money, the poor don't. America gives money because it is afraid of Communism. Whatever America has spent on India could have built a new India if it had been used properly. If America didn't help,

we'd be forced to help ourselves. The big businessmen buy up
stocks of food and other commodities and create shortages. "We
know that America will never stop giving us aid," they say.
They're afraid India will join the Russians. Here's an example.
The government wants to build a dam. Everybody involved takes
something. They'll use mud instead of cement. Everyone takes
bribes. If America doesn't help, then Russia will step in. If Russia
helps a revolt the government will not dare to complain.

[What about Russia's invasion of Czechoslovakia?] I'd say that
Russians are no better than Americans. They have no right to interfere. The Russians are not really Communists. They might have
been forty years ago, but not now. Today they are capitalists. The
scientists, the bureaucrats, get special privileges. The Russians in
the embassy here are all corrupt. They deal in the black market,
and buy things in India that aren't available in Russia and sell
them when they go home.

[On the drug scene, which is just beginning to touch well-to-do
young people in the universities.] People take drugs because of
frustration. They don't have any real problems. They've got
money and all the modern amenities. Suppose I'm living in
America—all the facilities, a hell of a lot of money, four or five
children, but I ignore them. I'm happy but the younger generation
is frustrated. They don't get affection from the parents, they feel
avoided. It's better in India. No, on second thought it isn't. The
poor people take drugs. So do the university students. People who
take drugs are not generally happy. "Would you like a joint?" "I
wouldn't mind." Once, not more than that for me. Whenever you
want to run away from the realities and the facts of life, that's when
you take drugs. Everybody lacks something. A person who has
money may need affection. I have a friend, a very very intelligent
person whose parents were divorced. He was living with his
mother. He writes poetry, directs plays. He started taking charas
[a form of marijuana]. He's given up his studies. Another friend—
his mother died when he was seven and his father remarried—the

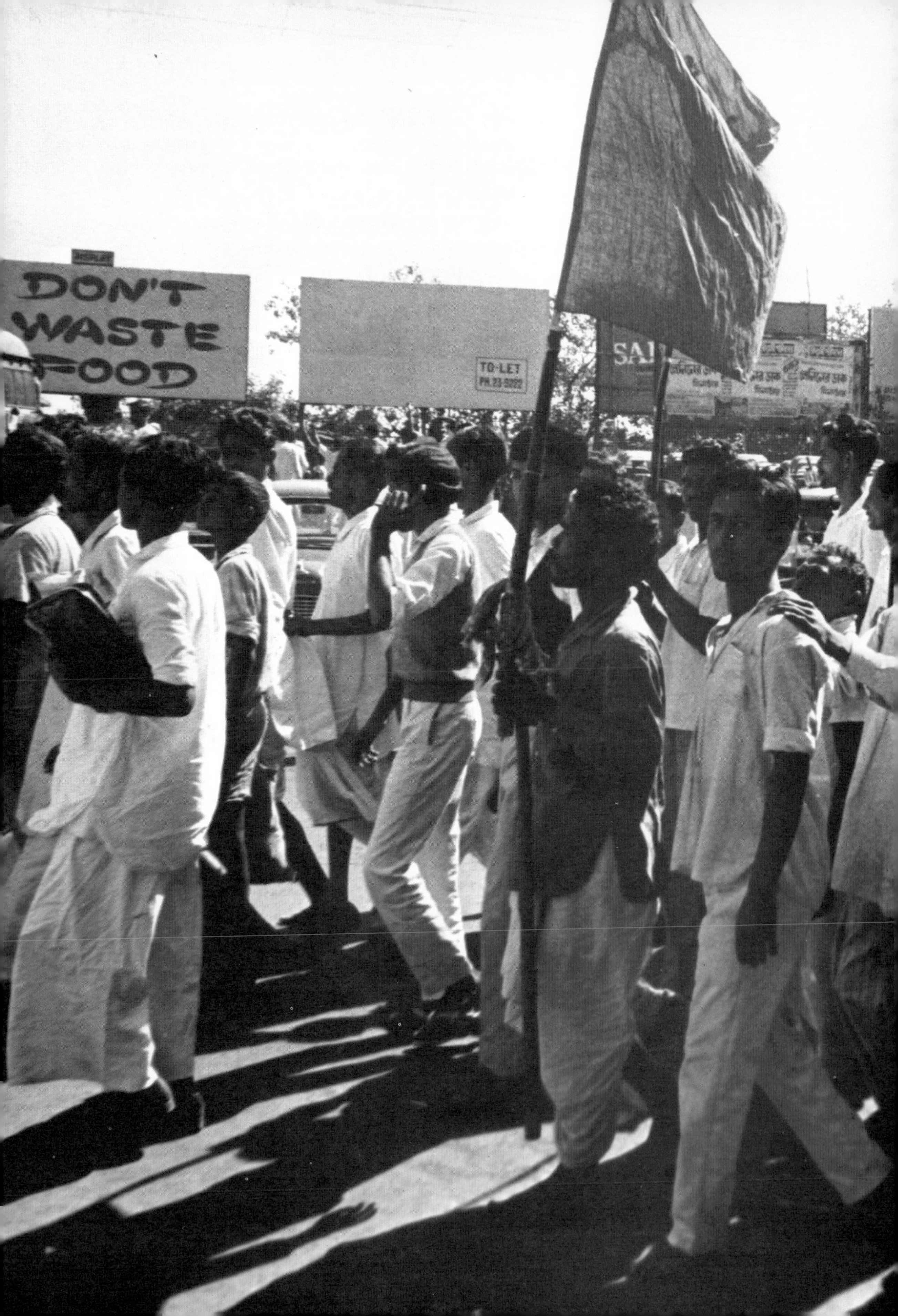
DON'T WASTE FOOD
TO-LET

stepmother treats him like dirt. Every time I meet him he's stoned. Girls are taking drugs at the U. There must be something missing somewhere.

India is in trouble. Nobody can help us—a Hitler, the Americans. If anyone tries to interfere, we'll kick him out. A military dictatorship is possible. There is a limit to everything, a limit to patience, to suffering. There are people who are working actively. We've had some local peasant revolts. They didn't succeed and the people were beaten up and had to flee. But something will happen.

Vietnam is a horrible thing. The Americans haven't got any right to be there. India is one percent capitalist, and if the other ninety-nine percent start a revolution, the one percent will invite the Americans to put it down. That will be wrong. In capitalism ten percent oppress ninety percent, in Communism it's the other way. Whatever the masses want should be done.

[He tells me a dream.] Many times I have dreamed that snakes have bitten me. I asked an astrologer and he says it means my friends might be thinking ill of me and want to harm me. That's why I dream of snakes. But I don't think he's right, though I've dreamt of snakes many times.

I know a lady—she was living in her village—just moved back there—every night she used to dream that a skeleton was walking towards her and wanted to choke her and kill her. Every night she used to get very nervous, thinking of her dreams, and she became very weak. So this lady and her husband approached the village elders about the dreams. They told her that forty or fifty years ago the person who makes certain kinds of oils had lived in her house and was murdered by robbers and was buried in her room. That same night they dug in the floor and found the skeleton.

[On Sunday, along with Mrs. Q., an English woman who has come to India in an attempt to sell a gigantic and distasteful metal statue of Gandhi to the government—she expected to get $40,000 —we go for a drive to see some of his father's property. The family has farms in several places and a village. It seems to be "his" village. The villagers treat him with great respect, but I have the impression they would like to kill him. The revolution may be closer than Kakoo believes. He walks around like a little prince, giving orders and making everyone jump. The headman tries to ignore him. He had said he had to be back in New Delhi by one in the afternoon to see a friend, but the hours go by. I remind him of his appointment. "Oh, he'll wait." On the way home he begins to talk about marriage.]

One must respect one's parents. You've got to do what they want. After all, what does a young person know about life, marriage, another person? I don't believe in love marriages. The parents know best. They can look at the young people and make a proper match. Love doesn't last long. You have your whole life ahead of you and if you are young you can make a mistake. Yes, let the parents decide. [Kakoo asks if America has the joint family system. I say no, and explain about young people having the right to their own households.] I still prefer the Indian system. When your parents get old, it's the duty of the children to support them. The joint family is better.

He has no idea of what he will do in the future, except to go to college and the university as long as possible. He decides he can't go to Switzerland because "honorable ministry has imposed more restrictions." He is erratic, opinionated, fairly well-informed. He knows about the Beatles, the Rolling Stones, Harry Belafonte, who are all imitated by rock groups at the University. Late one afternoon we are sitting in the courtyard of the house in New Delhi. There is a slight breeze and a servant brings us oranges, tea and crackers. Mrs Q. begins to talk about her husband, who has been studying astrology for six years. Recently he has given up traditional methods of interpretation and has developed a psychological method. Mrs. Q. says, for example, that her husband can tell if you are afraid of drowning, just from your stars, and what to do about it.

Kakoo: "Stay out of the water."
Mrs. Q.: "No, learn to swim."

Changing India

Prabhakar
Narayan Mohite

MESSENGER, Age 19

Prabhakar Narayan Mohite is one of the people cast adrift by the changes in India. He doesn't know where he is going. He lives in a single room with his mother and three younger brothers; a number of other people wander in and out, and it is hard to tell if they are relatives or neighbors. Their tenement is just one of many in central Bombay. The streets outside are full of villagers who have come en masse from the countryside to Bombay to enjoy a better kind of life. They have retained enough of their traditions to keep them together. But Prabhakar is lost. He works as a *peon* or messenger, bouncing around from one office to another, and isn't really sure what he wants to do. Now nineteen, he has been in Bombay less than a year, having grown up in a village called Kankavali, in Maharashtra state, where he was educated up to the tenth grade. This is more schooling than most young Indians receive. Prabhakar says he can read both Marathi and English and follows the newspapers in both languages, though when I spoke to him in English he froze and I had to ask Mrs. Pandit to translate. Mrs. Pandit, who introduced me to Prabhakar, said, "He knows a little about the world, but the world is getting so complicated that it is difficult for him to keep track of everything."

Money is not the only criteria of being rich. Mental riches are more important. [What are mental riches?] Better human relations, being nice to people, mixing with them, talking to them. I've been through the tenth standard. Now I'd like to go to night school and get my certificate. I don't know what I want to be, perhaps a clerk. But I like painting and drawing. I look at pictures and try to copy them. I wish I could study art but I have to pass the regular scholastic examinations. I really don't do much painting. The materials are expensive. It's sort of a dream.

I came to Bombay nine months ago. I work as a *peon* in an office but I don't think I'll stay. I've been in different places. You can't get a job unless you're eighteen. I'm nineteen now. I like Bombay better than Kankavali. My mother was born here and works as a tea woman in a municipal school. My brothers go to school here. My father was a ticket taker in a movie house but he drank himself to death. He was thirty-five; I was seven when he died. We are Marathis, warriors in the old days. That's our caste. We conquered half of India. People were afraid of us. The caste system is being modified. No more warriors and fighting men—we're now farmers and *peons*. It's not right.

I grew up in Kankavali with my grandfather but I used to come to Bombay to see my parents. If I don't go to school here I may go back to Kankavali. It would be good to have a farm. I could raise rice and sugar cane, cereals and lentils. You can rotate all the crops but the cane. I have no plans for getting married now, but if I had a farm I'd need a wife who can help. I'd like a girl who is educated but is still willing to work in the fields, someone who knows both Bombay and village life.

Having a farm might be better than an office job. There is no future here. It is not possible to work your way up. India is such a poor country. There are rich people, but still it is a poor country. Take the riots in Bombay—thousands of people were hurt, the damage ran into millions of rupees. I don't know the real cause— they said it was over language problems—but it could be because of poverty. Riots are bad because we have to replace everything. We have riots because the world isn't as good as it should be. I suppose riots help solve problems because they make people aware that they exist. I read the newspapers and know what is going on. There is trouble all over the world. [Would you go to another country?] Give me the address and I will go. America, that is the place. Great discoveries; they'll help us get to know new things. I'm not afraid of going to a strange country, not afraid of the noise, the buildings, the subways. I haven't seen American movies (I prefer Indian films) but I read about America in geography books in school.

It was better under the British. People talk that way. Discipline, enough food, lower prices. Now India is all shaken up. It's too expensive. I'd like to have a few things—a radio, a watch, clothes, western style clothes. I don't like Indian clothes. I wouldn't wear them.

Can you get me a job in America?

There is a strong sense of pride and a touch still of the military air in Marathi caste people. One afternoon Prabhakar and Miss Lal and I were walking through the streets near his house. We came across a wedding which was being held in the street. The bride and groom were sitting in the center of the roadway, looking very grim, while hundreds of village women sat all around them making ribald remarks and having a great frolicking party. I stopped to take photographs, and suddenly there was a Cosmic Encounter unfolding. The women began to pose

and flirt and to say things they knew I couldn't understand. As I grew more deeply involved in the photographs, Prabhakar became very angry: my time and friendship were his for the afternoon, not theirs, and finally, in order to keep peace with him, I gave up the wedding. But his anger was real and justified. His eyes flashed and when I took some pictures of him and his brothers on the roof of his house he was still smoldering.

We went back to the street with Miss Lal. Prabhakar steered us away from the wedding. I asked him what he thought of Mrs. Gandhi. "Oh, she's all right." Then he added, "But she embarrasses me."

Shashi Kanta

SCHOOLGIRL, Age 15

From time to time as one walks through the streets of Anangpur, a small, solidly constructed village in Haryana state which lies west of New Delhi on the Ganges plain, one hears the sharp crack of anti-aircraft guns. Above the village sleeve targets float past, towed by clumsy planes of the Indian Air Force. Flak has fallen on the village. Five people were known to have been killed shortly before I visited Anangpur, and there were rumors of other deaths. The villagers had tried to bring charges, but the Air Force refused to accept them. Many of the people are quarry workers and are desperately poor. Some go into target areas (bombs are dropped too) to pick up copper fragments to sell. Always on the verge of starvation, they kill their troubles with toddy made of sugar, which is sometimes spiced with a lizard. The lizard is believed to heighten intoxication: one theory is that the lizards are poisonous and that a slight touch of the poison increases the effect of the toddy, just as hippy chemists in America will add a touch of rat poison to LSD for a quicker high.

There is bootlegging of toddy into New Delhi. The police put up roadblocks, but these (someone says in the village) are merely to force bribes out of the smugglers. The police are poor, too.

Anangpur's mud and stone houses make it appear slightly better off than many villages on the plain. It has a new school building, but the roof has collapsed six months after it was completed and the building stands empty. It is the usual problem of the contractor using cheap materials and not enough reinforcements. Anangpur, which was named after a former ruler, is believed to be a thousand years old. It was founded at a time when the West was just coming out of the Dark Ages, an era when India was equal to and perhaps better than Europe in culture, economy and living standards. Today Anangpur is virtually owned by a few wealthy families from New Delhi, who are constructing summer houses on the outskirts.

It is Sunday. Shashi Kanta, who is fifteen, and her brother Rajesh, thirteen, and their father, O. P. Gupta (he adds, "M.A., P.E.S."—Indians are fond of stating their qualifications), the principal of the village school, are seated on the verandah with some children and a few adults. The verandah faces a huge courtyard which is dry and dusty. One side of the yard is formed by the ruined addition to the school. Flies buzz around us; overhead is the regular thud-thud of the anti-aircraft shells. On the road outside the school a small caravan of camels pulls itself together and the bad tempered animals shuffle down the road, puffing and snorting and showing every sign of their fury with the world. The heat is intense, but since the humidity is low it is bearable. However, everything seems parched. The ink in my pen dries out every day and I must constantly refill it. The past week has been frightfully hot, but one morning there was a sudden rain storm that dropped the thermometer to 85°. Everyone felt the cold. The women wrapped themselves in winter shawls. After prolonged exposure to the heat of the plain even I felt chilly. Now it is hot again. The dust sweeps across the compound and Shashi begins to talk about herself.

I want to become a doctor. Indian medicine is sweeter, western medicine is bitter [she is referring to the taste]. All my brothers would like to be doctors, too. It would be a great thing.

[Her father interrupts and says in English, "It is impossible for a village teacher to educate his children as doctors. It's too expensive. Perhaps we can get her into ayurvedic medicine."]

We are Banyas [a business caste]. We don't mix with the sweepers, but the classes in school are mixed. The little children, sweepers, cobblers, the higher castes, all play together. [In some schools low caste and untouchable children sit on the school verandah and hear their lessons through the window of the classroom.] I believe in a democratic way of life. But I couldn't marry someone from another caste. I must go by my father's wish. Here in Anangpur the village girls marry at ten and twelve. My father comes from another village where they marry at fifteen and sixteen. But the more education a girl has the later the age of marriage. After the university, when I am twenty-three or twenty-four my father will find a husband for me. [Mr. Gupta interjects: "She has put very much trust in her mother. Whatever her mother says, she will do." The mother has had some education.]

I've seen some movies on our village television set. Some day each village will have television. Now we have one or two movies a month. I also see movies at Faridabad and sometimes when I visit my uncle in New Delhi. They're all Indian movies, no foreign. But I do know about America and India—Mrs. Gandhi is the Prime Minister.

There is no temple here—we have to go to another village to worship—but my mother has a small shrine in the house. She does the worshipping. We are devotees of Hanuman [the monkey god]. He has become our *Isht Dev*. [Indians select one god or another as the *Isht Dev*, or a personal god.]

[Dream] If I have heard of a horrifying thing during the day, I

may dream of it at night. Sometimes I dream of animals I have seen during the day.

[Rajesh, who would also like to be a doctor "to help the poor," says he has a dream. He has dreamed of a snake, but he is unable to report any details. Mr. Gupta interjects: "At one time the snake was worshipped. Now we respect him. We don't kill snakes."]

[Another student, who is sitting with us, wants to tell his dream. He is Bhaj Raj, the son of a teacher at the school. He would like to become a headmaster. He has never seen a movie, though he has watched the village television set. He has never been anywhere, not even to New Delhi which can be reached by a few hours on a bus. His dream: "I saw a person with big pointed teeth and I was scared. Someone told me a story like that."]

Shashi is a slight, serious girl in *salwar* and *kurta,* the traditional dress in this area. She has very clear ideas about her place in the family and her role vis-à-vis the parents. She has not spoken unless spoken to, but now we have become friends and she opens up cautiously. "I feel a kind of joy," she says when I ask her what she thinks of all the questions I have been putting to her. I am the first foreigner she has met and it pleases her to know that I am interested in her life. "What is education like in America?" she asks. "Is there any punishment?" She'd like to know the attitudes of students and teachers to each other. I explain that it is very open. "Here we hardly speak to the teacher," she says, the teacher being a figure of authority, even with his low wages. Mr. Gupta remarks that "Give and take, that is the best method of education." He seems sad when he says this, because it is not his way of teaching, and if he were to attempt it, he would be severely criticized.

He tells me that Shashi is the third of four children. "All are alive. Since thirteen years we have been practicing family planning." Then he takes me to see his house. The family lives in a small compound behind the school. The tiny court is crowded with stacks of wood and broken furniture, but the rest of the house is neat and clean. "It is a dream, this wanting to be a doctor," he says. "All my children are dreamers. We must face the facts. It is a tragedy, it is too expensive."

Shashi doesn't know what her father is saying. She speaks Punjabi and Hindi, and though she has learned a little English in school and says she can understand a few words of what I have been saying, she cannot follow a rapid conversation in English. "I will have to stop them. It is too expensive. I may be able to get her into ayurvedic medicine, but western no. Impossible." He is sad that Shashi, so bright and forward looking, will not be able to become a doctor. But she will continue to think, for a long time, that she can.

Overhead the ack-ack bursts in tiny puffs and molten bits of lead fall on the outlying farms. It is a subtle kind of war, the ruling classes with their western games which mean only death and taxes to the people on the plain.

Ashoka

ELEPHANT BOY, Age 17

Sometimes India reminds me of the ocean. It looks like one great undifferentiated mass of people, like so many identical waves. To the tourists who jump from Calcutta to the Taj Mahal in Agra and then to Bombay, it is. All Indians look the same, just as all Americans must look the same to a foreigner on a five day visit. But soon, even quickly, people separate into cultures and groups and families, into tribes and languages, into light and dark, simple, sophisticated, gentle, sweet, friendly, rascally or opportunist. Many groups are never seen, even by other Indians. Quite by chance I heard about a group of tribals in southern Mysore, jungle people who antedate the early Aryan warriors who swept over India. In a very broad sense the tribals are the equivalent of the American Indian, original inhabitants who were pushed back and partially destroyed by foreign invaders. There are many types of tribals, from the small dark people who resemble the Australian bushmen, to many who seem no different from the average Indian, to others who are definitely Mongol in type and are related to the Far Eastern races. The Aryans drove the tribals out of the plains and into the recesses of the jungles; they lost their homes, farms and ways of life. Many of the survivors still live in the jungles, as hunters and nomads. Some are quite wild, and others have made clearings and are farmers. They have had to survive in what was once a hostile environment. Though originally animists and spiritualists, a number of tribals were converted to Hinduism (a process that is still continuing, with resistance), and many to Christianity. But tribal life is still vital and strong. There are fifty million tribals—nearly ten percent of India —but they are in effect separate nations, with customs, religion, desires that make them quite unlike their Hindu masters.

The tribals I was told about are elephant people. As far back as any one can remember, they have taken care of elephants. They understand elephants as no one else does. They grow up with elephants, and the elephants with them. They are so skilled with elephants that when the British wanted to use elephants in Burma, they sent some of this particular group of tribals, the Korubas, to Burma, where they still live in the jungle with their elephants.

The elephant is a way of life in the great forests of southern India. The jungles are heavy and dense: they are thick with flowers, snakes, birds, wild creatures of all kinds, rare woods, teak and rosewood and other great heavy trees that can bring as much as $7,000 for a large full-grained straight log. Elephants root them out and pull them down. Only an elephant can do this properly. Machines could be used, but they damage the wood, and the elephant is far superior. He can move on cat feet through the jungle, hardly bruising a fern, but when he is coming back from a hard day's work, on his way down to the river, he emerges with a joyous crash that lets everyone know his day is finished and now he's going to have his bath.

At this point the elephant's keeper, the mahout, turns his elephant over to a boy, the khotal, whose job it is to care for the elephant. Often the khotal will be the son of a mahout. Elephants are relaxed and gentle, but when mistreated they can be mean and difficult. Of all animals, elephants are the easiest to train in adulthood—one might even say, to civilize—and they are the most human in their responses and intelligence. They suffer from indigestion and the common cold, are affectionate, friendly, and warm in their personal relationships, with each other and with people, and form undying attachments with those they love.

Late one afternoon I go to the waterhole with some friends of mine and a local Indian who speaks Hindi and Kanada, the common language in the area, to see if we can find an elephant boy willing to talk to us. We watch the elephants coming down to the water. They are in the charge of teenage boys, though some of them are being led by children who seem barely old enough to toddle. The earth shakes, but the tiny children run fearlessly beneath the elephants' feet.

One teenage boy seems particularly bright in the way he handles his elephant. Govind, the local man, calls him over. He comes reluctantly. His name is Karea. His father is a mahout, but Karea only bathes the elephants. He is thirteen now, and has been helping care for elephants for the last three years. He doesn't go to school, and hangs around the village during the day when the elephants are working. Suddenly he bolts away.

"He thinks you are a government inspector and are going to report him," says Govind. "Tribals are very shy," says one of the people with me. "They just go."

Another boy has been watching us covertly as he washes his elephant. When he is finished, he turns his elephant over to one of the children, calmly goes to a bush where he removes his wet clothes and puts on a white shirt and black shorts, and walks by us. He seems very apprehensive, but obviously he wants us to talk to him. Then he sits down about ten feet away. Meanwhile elephants are walking back and forth close to us, shaking the earth and towering above us like great trees. It is somewhat unnerving, because I had been told earlier in the day about a wild elephant who had cornered a man and his son and killed them.

Later it occurred to me that the victims were Indians and not tribals. Govind begins to talk to the boy. He is straight and slim, with dark skin and regular features. He is a little nervous, but courageous. What he tells us soon indicates a daring as unusual as if an American teenager had gone off to the moon unprepared.

> There are twenty-five of us in our village. We have six elephants to care for; they belong to the government, but we are the mahouts. There is another village twenty miles away. We are clearing land and bringing in timber. When the job is done here we will move to another spot.
>
> My father is a mahout. My name is Ashoka [after a famous Indian emperor]. We are all members of the Koruba tribe, a sub-caste of the Sudras. We Korubas stay together. We know the jungle and the animals and the other jungle people, and we stay away from outsiders. I've never seen a light-skinned person before, either. That's why I came over to you; I was curious.
>
> Until three years ago I had never been outside the forest. When I was fourteen I decided I wanted to be a forest ranger. So I got a few paise [about one or two cents] and walked out of the jungle and along a dirt road and then on the paved road to the village where the bus stops, and I took the bus to Coorg, which is 27 miles from here, and enrolled in the Forest Rangers School. I am in the third standard. I am learning to read and write in Kanada [the tribals' own language is unwritten], though I cannot read the newspapers yet. I've passed all my examinations and next year I will enter the fourth standard. It's a twelve year course. The school was established by the government to help the tribals. It's free—everything—classes, meals, the room. We get no money, but there is plenty of food. Here we eat ragi [a millet] which we cook in hot water with vegetables, but in school there is rice, lentils and coffee. Sometimes we see movies and there is a radio at the school.

His knowledge of the world is woefully inadequate. He says that he learns things in school, like the name of the Prime Minister, which he forgets when he returns to the jungle. The entire course takes twelve years—he will be 26 when he finishes—but he is not sure his parents will allow him to continue. They may want him to marry a girl from another Koruba village. If he is fortunate, the parents will let him return to school after marriage.

The jungle is his life: he knows the paths, the animals, the course of the seasons, the other tribals, who when together are not shy but uproariously gregarious. And above all he knows the great friendly elephants, who are his brothers and his gods.

Our god is Ganpatti, the elephant god. [He is usually known as Ganesh elsewhere.] We put pictures of him in a shrine in our homes, with coconuts and flowers, and then we do *puja* [worship]. As I see pictures of the gods, so do I dream. Sometimes the animals come to bite me, then I kill them. Otherwise I just sit and look. Once Ganpatti was angry [in a dream], once he came to help. But he is our god. Ganpatti is the elder son of Shiva, the lord of the Universe. We pray to him when we begin something. Ganpatti is the god of wisdom and prudence, very cheerful and fat from eating good food.

[I ask Ashoka what he would like most in the world. He thinks for a long time.] Mangoes and fruit, things like that.

He tells me that with the information I have and the photographs I have taken, I'll go abroad and tell other people what the Korubas are like. He says he wasn't nervous. When he first sat down, Govind asked him, "Are you going to be frightened like the other boy and run away?" he replied, "No, I'm not scared."

He tells me that his father, Gedja Mistry, is a good man, and so is his mother a good woman. He has a sister ten, and one nineteen, but obviously the ages mean nothing, and Govind is merely guessing when he translates. Then Ashoka picks up his wet clothes, signals in some way to an elephant, steps on the curled trunk and is swung up on the elephant's back and rides away.

Vasudeo

APPRENTICE MECHANIC, Age 19

An Indian factory or store rarely resembles the American pattern, though there are some mills and industries on a western scale with tens of thousands of workers, which are impressively as good as or better than those in Europe and the United States. I was once taken to a "big" toy factory in Benares, which turned out to be three aged craftsmen working on the floor (the toys were beautiful). Most enterprises, factories, shops, businesses consist of a single man and his son or sons, or a craftsman with an apprentice or two and a worker who follow a way of working common to their caste and one which the caste has practiced for many generations. Today, besides the traditional factories and shops of metal workers, cobblers, bakers, rope spinners, weavers, millers, carpenters, shoemakers and all the other assorted tiny in-

dustries that form the bottom and middle layers of Indian village and urban life, there are new enterprises for the modern world, like the numerous bicycle and auto repair shops found off the main roads and streets. Vasudeo, who is nineteen, follows the traditional system but in a modern context, as an auto mechanic. He works as a helper in a small repair shop on the outskirts of New Delhi. There is another apprentice, Attar Singh, who is a year older. Vasudeo (he has no family name), as a mechanic, represents the generation that is sliding between two worlds, moving from a rural agricultural background into the industrial world in a manner that represents the loosening of traditional modes of living and traditional attitudes. He is mildly alienated from his roots, but even with his worries and anxieties, he is making progress. He is certainly being stirred to some ambition. He would like to have his own shop, and does not mind talking about it in front of his boss.

I was born in a village called Kotla Mubarakpur. My father is a farmer, both dairy and agriculture. The village is only a mile from here. Now it is part of New Delhi. That's how fast things are going today. The whole world is changing. My father had to buy some land further out—it's thirteen miles from here. He grows wheat, gram and millet. He's tried some of the new seeds [various foreign agencies have attempted to introduce fast-growing wheat and rice]. They're better than the old ones. He's producing a lot more. But I suppose the new farm, too, will be swallowed up by the city.

We have thirteen people in our house [a joint family]: I have six brothers—one is away and one is in the army—and three sisters. I am the third eldest child. I still haven't seen my father's farm. He goes there every day. I work here six days a week, from nine in the morning to seven at night. My boss gives me tea and snacks. I earn sixty rupees a month. My father takes it and gives me back ten. It's not enough.

I'm an apprentice. I began three years ago. One year without pay and then I got paid. I do auto repairs. I can repair brakes, do a ring job, work like that. I help the mechanic [one of the co-owners of the shop]. I'd like to have my own place. I'd like to have a better job. I'd quit but so far I haven't looked. I like it here—the boss is good. I respect him and he respects me. So I am satisfied.

I can't go back to the farm. That's my father's life but not mine. He's doing all right. But from an agricultural point of view, India isn't. She's having trouble. There's not enough food. We've got rationing and all kinds of controls. It's the population that makes us poor. There are other factors but it's mainly population. I don't know what kind of future India has. Who can say? There is no definite answer. My immediate reaction is that people are likely to starve. I mean real starvation, not the kind of marginal starving we've been having. But India will survive, she always has [a common remark]. Mrs. Gandhi? She's all right. But that's all. I really don't have any opinion of her. I can't vote yet, so I'm not political. That will come later.

[The boss arrives. Vasudeo and Attar Singh give him their seats and stand. The boss immediately begins to tell me his life story, which is a combination of hard luck and ambition and success. He says he comes from the area which is now West Pakistan. Since his family is Hindu they had to flee. He was only a child then. In the north he had to learn Urdu, then in India, Punjabi and Hindi, all three of which are closely related. He is now twenty-six or twenty-seven (age is again vague) but he looks forty. He gave up school and became an apprentice in a garage and worked his way up. He and his two partners have had the repair shop five years. He has plenty of work but not enough equipment. An Indian sociologist, Mrs. Kussim Nair, has written that people like the boss who have been forcibly transposed to another area always do better than settled people. The boss sends Attar Singh out for cola drinks.]

[I ask Vasudeo what caste he belongs to. He looks distressed.] I am a Gujar. It is a farming caste [one of the lowest]. We don't eat meat or drink alcohol, my family, but . . . well. My older brother drinks alcohol. I'd eat meat often but it's expensive. I'm not fussy about food. I eat non-vegetarian [the standard euphemism for meat]. My brother in the Army eats meat to keep healthy. My father supports the idea although he doesn't eat meat himself.

People are vegetarians because of religious sentiments.

I've been married since I was sixteen to a girl from Uttar Pradesh. The proposal came from her parents. She's visiting them now but normally she lives in our household. We were engaged a year before we were married. We don't have any children yet—we practice family planning. Sometimes I go by bus to see my wife's family. They live not far from here, but you know, I haven't seen any other parts of New Delhi. Lived here all my life, too. I had six years of schooling—I can read—but never have the time. I'd rather go to the movies. I go every Sunday, oftener if I can. My family doesn't like it. My father wants me to save my money. I listen to the radio at home. My brother has a small transistor. That's why I know the Americans are going to the moon. They give arms to India, and wheat. [He has heard the name Vietnam but doesn't know the context.] I see Americans here—they go by in the cars and motorbicycles. They've got funny clothes. Some of them wear Indian clothes, but they don't fit properly and look funny. Very.

[Dreams] I don't dream. I have daydreams of getting my driver's license and opening up my own shop.

[Attar Singh tells me about his dreams. He was married when he was ten but his wife didn't come to live with him until he was eighteen. Now they have a five-month-old girl. "I dream that I am pedalling a scooter to start it. Sometimes I dream about my work."]

Would Vasudeo like to go to America? "Yes, yes." He smiles. "As a mechanic. It would be a good life. I'd be a mechanic and have my own shop. A mechanic!"

Lucia Damor

TRIBAL, Age 18

Like any aboriginal people who were pushed back by foreigners who not only coveted their lands but feared them, the tribals of India were described as evil spirits and near-animals by the people who had robbed and persecuted them. The tribals' "sins" and strange customs were given as justification for the robbery. The tribals were elusive, canny, full of wiles and dangerous. A Sanskrit poem written about the seventh century gives some of the reasons for the enmity, which is said to exist still among contemporary Indians.

> Their life is a hallucination
> of ignorance and errors,
> their conduct is censored by honorable men,

their religion is the offering of human flesh,
their food is meat, and they drink spirits,
which are condemned by honorable men.

Their exercise is hunting,
their hymns the howls of jackals,
their wisdom the knowledge of the
ways of the birds.

Their friends are dogs,
their kingdoms the wild woods.

Drinking bouts are their festivities,
their helpers are merciless bows,
their tools snake-like arrows
with poisonous heads.

Their songs are a lure for the deer,
their wives are women
captured from other tribes.

Tigers are their companions.
The blood of animals
are their offering to the gods.

Their sacrifice is flesh.

Their livelihood is robbery.

Their ornaments are snakes,
their cosmetics pus
from the wounds of elephants.

In every way they devastate
the forests
where they dwell.

The Aryans had a superstitious dread of the jungle peoples, and with the enmity of the conqueror for the people he has despoiled, practiced a kind of apartheid which had the effect of saving the aborigines. The tribals were isolated until the last century, when the modern world began to erode their way of life. Missionaries, both Hindu and

Christian, began to proselytize them. Some tribals have been persuaded to take jobs in the large steel mills in eastern India, others move back and forth from the jungles to the cities and eventually become part of the depressed urban proletariat, losing roots and hope. A few people, Indians and foreigners, have become sufficiently interested in the tribals to live among them and to try to help them. Some have been doctors, others missionaries. P., a European, spent twenty years among the Bhils, a tribal group in eastern India, and has a great affection for them. Now he runs a center of classical music and dancing in the hills north of Bombay and has some Bhils among the students. The center, Gyan Ashram, which is affiliated with the University of Lucknow, was originally planned as a secluded retreat for study and meditation (it is both a school and an *ashram* or spiritual abode), but the city is gradually encroaching upon it. Overhead one sees and hears international jets going into Bombay's Santa Cruz airport. A major highway now runs a mile from the *ashram,* and there is a minor macadam road along one edge of its lands. The school has several hundred day students and about two dozen resident students (among them the Bhils), who not only study but farm a small vegetable garden, do the cooking and some manual labor as a part of their curriculum. Normally much of this work would be done by servants.

The classes are held in a large, spacious brick and concrete building which has classrooms and separate rooms for study and practice; there are several smaller buildings for the same purposes. Meals are taken in a large wall-less tin-roofed shelter with an open kitchen in one wing.

We have just had lunch—rice, lentils in curry, chappatis and fruit. The students sit around the edges of the shelter on mats with their tin plates in front of them. P., some young Germans who have come from Europe by VW bus, Miss Lal and I are at a small table. The students and their teachers clean up and go off to practice. The sound of sitars, tablas —the twin drums that are a basic unit of Indian music—and harmonium comes from the different buildings. Though each student is playing his own instrument and melody, the sounds complement each other more than they conflict. The long bamboo leaves rustle slightly;

birds fly through the enclosure, and bees hum through the lush plants that remain from the jungle. It is very pleasant. Off to one side, four Bhil girls are stringing necklaces in traditional tribal patterns, which will be sold to help the school.

P. begins to talk about the Bhils. He is a large relaxed man who has become an Indian citizen and wears a *dhoti* and *kurta*. "They're a wild, tough people," he says. "They don't live in villages like the Hindu and Muslim peasants but scattered in the jungle, each house with a small clearing. The houses are made of thatch covered with mud. As an experiment we got some of them to build brick houses but they broke down the windward walls and replaced them with thatch. Keeps the house cooler. Most of the Bhils have small gardens planted with maize [Indian corn, which tastes like pebbles even when cooked], but they're still primarily hunters. The basic diet is animals and fish.

"They're rugged. Very strong. We're doing some building here. The peasant coolies can carry only ten bricks each but a Bhil girl will carry thirty without thinking of it. Back in the jungle they're great drinkers. They make alcohol out of a flower called 'mauva'. It's a very malodorous tree. After it's boiled it can be drunk in half an hour. It's a naturally alcoholic drink. Even the animals get drunk by eating mauva that have fallen on the ground. Tigers eat it and get drunk. Every Bhil is a natural distiller. They drink heavily to drown their sorrows, and when they drink, they dance.

"They're violent, too. It must be the centuries of being repressed in the jungle and the hardships. A lot of murders in the Bhil areas. Some of them are professional robbers. I remember a case when some Bhils stole four bullocks and disappeared. There wasn't a trace of them."

Since the Bhils are spread out all over the jungle, they send messages by drum: a tiger in the area, strangers or robbers coming, the announcement of a wedding or a birth or a death. The drums are big and powerful but can convey the most delicate sounds and rhythms. (The Bhils shout to close neighbors instead of drumming.)

The Bhils have no caste system, but are separated into families and clans; the old women are the genealogists and keep track of the complicated structure of relationships. Other aborigines who were unable to escape the Aryans found themselves either among the Sudras, the fourth caste, or the untouchables, but the Bhils were able to keep separate. Now, though they have tried to keep their ancient ways, the Bhils are being forced to change. They are becoming both Hinduized and westernized in varying degrees. There is confusion about their basic religious beliefs, whether they are animists or monotheists, or if they practice the original primordial Hinduism untouched by the additions brought by the Aryans. Both Hindu and Christian missionaries have been converting them to their respective beliefs, but the most independent and obstinate among the Bhils say they have their own idea of God and don't want to be Hindus or Christians. The Bhil girls in the school are Christian and are in a half-way state into the larger world. Miss Lal and I and a Bhil girl named Lucia Damor go for a walk around the *ashram* and then sit underneath a huge rambling tree with gnarled branches and twisted roots and talk.

I am eighteen now. I come from Panchkuin in Madhya Pradesh [a big state in eastern India]. I've been at Gyan Ashram for seven years. I'm studying tabla, singing, dancing, musical theory, English and Hindi. No mathematics. I have a younger sister and two older brothers. One of them is a farmer, the other a teacher. My father is an overseer on a farm run by an Indian priest from Kerela. My grandparents were converted to Christianity by the missionaries. In our area people are either Christian or Hindu or the old religion—it's a kind of animism, I'd say. There's hardly any intermarriage among the three. In fact, we really don't mix at all with each other. Each religion brings a different way of life. The Christians usually live in village groups instead of scattered through the jungle as we did in the past. We still speak our own language, which I guess you would call "Bhil." [After Lucia had said a few words in Bhil, Miss Lal says it sounds like Gujarati, one of the common major Indian languages, but it seems to be more primitive Aryan than Hindi.]

I went through the fifth grade at Panchkuin, but then I decided to come here because I wanted to learn classical Indian music. I'm very keen on classical music. Bhil music is simpler and we rely more on drums. But classical Indian music is exciting. I teach tabla as well as study it.

Four years ago we went to Europe, a group of singers and dancers and musicians from the *ashram*. I heard some western music, some of the great classics, Bach and Mozart and Beethoven—I can hardly remember the names now—but it doesn't mean much to me. We were gone for a full year—Belgium, Austria, Holland, Switzerland, Germany. We stayed in hotels and convents and with families. The people were friendly, but I didn't care for the food. It was so different. I was glad to come back. A year is a long time. I went home to Panchkuin and it was wonderful.

[I tried to find out if she had any problems of adjusting. Young Indians who have spent time abroad invariably do. Returning home can be a serious traumatic shock, but Lucia settled down in India as if she had never been away.]

When I finish here, I'll be a teacher. I don't know where I will teach, perhaps at home among my people, but I'll go where I'm needed. What interests me is the spiritual quality of music. That's what I want to teach. It is the music itself that is important, not the place or the pay. I'm in no hurry to marry. The traditional Bhils and the Hindus have arranged marriages, but we Christian Bhils believe in love marriages. However, my work comes first. I've just been reading a book called "For Him"—it's in Hindi and it's about a girl who lives in a simple way and looks after people in a hospital and what her life is like. One must help people, and I can do it through music.

[The Question: who are you?] A Bhil girl. A Catholic girl. [She gets flustered and waits a long time before answering again.] A girl.

[Dreams] I have religious dreams. I see Mother Mary. I once had a dream I was going through my examinations and I saw Mother Mary in the sky and she helped me with my examination. Sometimes I dream of my home and family because I need them.

Lucia reads the newspapers, but she says she is not conscious of what is going on. She is absorbed by her music. Later in the day I watch her drumming. She is a slight, very serious, very quiet and indrawn girl. She drums as if her mind is miles away, half-way across India in the jungle with her people. The tigers are chewing on mauva blossoms and becoming wildly drunk, and the drums echo across the valleys. Her fingers are incredibly dextrous and roll across the tabla, around the edges and over the round black spot on the top of each with an incredible range of sound and rhythm. For a long time I sit on the floor and listen. The drumming goes on and on, and Lucia is lost in a world of her own, before the Aryan warriors invaded India and drove the gentle people into the jungles, to drink, robbery and murder.

Nirghaz
Fakir Mahhammad

MISS INDIA, Age 19

S ome aspects of Indian life are changing very quickly. When movies were first being made in India, only prostitutes played in them. Now girls from the better families are the stars, and a popular actor has a royalty all his own. The Indian beauty contest, too, is something recent. Nirghaz Fakir Mahhammad, who is nineteen, has just won the Miss India beauty contest sponsored by *Eve's Weekly,* a leading woman's magazine. She is scheduled to go to America for the Miss World contest later in the year. What made her appearance in the contest unusual, aside from the fact that Indian girls are sat upon by their families, is that she is a Muslim, and Muslim women are normally kept at home. Some never go out (a fact that creates vitamin deficiencies because of the lack of fresh air and sunshine), and are quite restricted.

They are rarely seen by men outside their families, and usually keep their heads covered, if not their faces. Substantial numbers of Muslim women still wear the bourkha, a veil which covers the face except for tiny eye slits. But Nirghaz is a representative of the new Indian woman, enlightened, educated, and progressive by traditional standards.

She is a tall, slim girl, with the delicate slightly awkward movements of a young deer. "Gazelle-like" is a phrase that quite accurately fits her. The most enduring impression I have of her is of a shy person, with an inner vitality that she is careful to control in the presence of a stranger, gracefully proper with the self-assurance that some shy people have, but still not very certain what to do with those long legs and fine slim hands.

She is a very sweet, gentle girl, and very serious. One sees girls like her by the dozen in the swank restaurants and cafés of the big cities, in groups of young people (single dating between a boy and a girl is not allowed), sipping soft drinks and cafe espresso, and going from one identical place to another in search of something to do. These are young India's swingers, but by American standards, very small-town and backward. But they are the only teenagers in India who enjoy what the West would call a normal adolescence. Every other young person is already part of the labor force, whether working or not.

Nirghaz has just graduated from a western-type school founded by American nuns (in India much upper-class education is given by foreign missionaries). The missionaries—today—rarely attempt to make converts. What they hope for, in educating the children of big businessmen and government officials, is to establish a group of literate, pro-western leaders who will at least be sympathetic to, if not actively in favor of, Christianity.

> Our family lives in Bangalore, though we originally came from Kutch in northern India. We are Muslims and still speak Urdu at home, with English and a little Tamil. My ancestors were converted from Hinduism. I don't know why, except that they were said to be widely read and made the choice after considering all the possibilities. My great-grandfather and my grandfather were cloth

merchants and came to Bangalore for business reasons. My father
—he just passed away [note: this is a real western euphemism,
picked up in school]—was a lawyer and businessman.

I know you're curious why it happens that a Muslim girl goes
into a beauty contest. It is unusual, but times are changing. One
has to change with the times. I've had some criticism, but I don't
see any harm. The theatre is different—I think the stage is something bad.

I entered some local contests and was runner-up in every one of
them. I really was surprised and thrilled when I was chosen Miss
India. A few years ago a Muslim girl would not even have entered
a beauty contest. But, as I said, times are changing. My sister Tas-
meen, who is twenty-one, won the Pears Soap beauty contest last
week in Bombay. She's going to the Far East.

But it's not a question of youthful rebellion. There is none in
India. Indian girls respect their parents, and boys do too. Our up-
bringing is completely different from yours. It's the kind of up-
bringing that matters in a child's life. We hear about the American
generation gap and wonder what is going on. There is no such
thing in India. I am very close to my mother. There's such a lack
of trust in America: the drugs, LSD, too much freedom. Children should be controlled until they are a certain age—some
mature quickly, some are always young. They're easily carried
away by emotions. When one can think freely, judge between the
good and bad, then they can make decisions. We don't have hippies
here [she wrinkles her nose]. I don't think about them at all. I see
foreign hippies once in a while. I like dignity, especially in a man.
The hippies are moving away from . . . They lead a different life
altogether. They think they're unique in their behavior. They like
to attract a lot of attention. I don't know any myself. I've never
met any. I never really thought about them until you asked.

We are Muslims. We try to steer a middle course, not too broad-
minded, not too narrow. I believe in both sides. I say my prayers,
but one must enjoy life. There are two types of Muslims—we are
Sunnis, the others are Shiahs, the kind you find in Persia. The dif-

ference is that each kind says different prayers and the Sunnis do not follow Ramadan [the yearly month-long fast]. I know that some Muslims complain about prejudice on the part of Hindus, but after all, President Husain was a Muslim. I know that all people are all alike, Muslims, Hindus, Catholics.

[I ask her about her religious practices.] Muslim women don't go to the mosque. They say their prayers at home. I've read the Koran several times [in Arabic]. We begin our studies of the Koran at the age of seven, for an hour a day. We were taught alone at home, though some children have Koranic studies at school. I often read the *Yaseen Sharieff* [a book of prayers and blessings]. I want prayer to become a part of my regular habits. I'm engaged to a Muslim boy from Mauritius. We met in Bangalore. I couldn't marry someone who is not a Muslim. I don't think it is a question of love marriages versus arranged marriages. It's whatever leads to happiness that counts. My sister is not engaged, but I think she will marry when she returns from Singapore. This will be an arranged marriage. My fiancé is studying to become a chartered accountant. He has to go abroad to finish his studies, and after we marry, we will live in Mauritius.

I went to mission schools—almost everyone does—to the Good Shepherd Convent and then to the Sacred Heart Girls High School. I was trained in all subjects except European languages. I finished teacher's training, but now I don't know—after marriage I'll stay at home and not teach and be a good wife for my husband. My education won't be wasted because I can teach my own children. Psychology can help you understand children's behavior.

[I ask her who she is.] I'm a girl. I'm Nirghaz. I'm my mother's daughter . . . because I love my mother. She's very understanding. I can talk to her freely.

[Dreams] Nothing. I don't dream . . . Well, I dream about being in a nursery teaching sweet little children. I teach them nursery rhymes. I guess I dream that particular way because during my teacher's training, at night I would think of the way I taught, the way I presented the lesson. I don't believe in horoscopes because I believe in Allah.

She stands up. She is amazingly tall, and even slighter than she had seemed while we were sitting and talking. She wears a pink *kurta* or blouse and very tightly fitted *churidars* in the style that is popular among chic young women in India and a long flowing pink scarf that runs across her throat and is draped behind her. "This is what I wear at home," says Nirghaz. "On the street I wear a sari."

We sit in the living room of her cousin's house where some friends of the cousin have dropped by out of curiosity to see Miss India. They are strangers to Nirghaz. They come from the same social stratum, but are without her grace and charm. I actually find them rather abrasive, but it could be their jealousy and uneasiness in her presence. Two are plump and catty and are wearing expensive but western dresses; the third is so plain that everyone ignores her. The girls offer to leave me off at my hotel. In the car they begin to chat about Miss India. "Reita Faria"—who was Miss India a few years previous—"was prettier. She had dark skin—I don't know why they gave it to a girl with dark skin—but she was prettier. Doesn't Nirghaz have bad skin!" I didn't want to be drawn into the conversation and merely grunted. "There were prettier girls in the contest, I'm sure. But that skin! Her father must have paid off the judges."

An Indian Lost,
an Indian Gained

Jacob Aptekar

EMIGRANT TO ISRAEL, Age 15

When St. Thomas the Apostle arrived in India in 55 A.D. at Cranganore on the Malabar coast of southern India, he was greeted by a Jewish girl playing the flute. He stayed in the Jewish quarter while beginning his mission to the Indians, which resulted in a group of converts known as St. Thomas Christians. There is doubt about the authenticity of St. Thomas, but none about the Jews, some of whom, from the evidence, have lived in India since the time of King Solomon, when they sailed his ships to the spice ports of India. Jews lived all along the western coast, with their colonies being refreshed from time to time by new immigrants, particularly from Babylon, Persia and Bagdad. Even as late as World War II there were new arrivals from Europe, who, however, stayed only briefly.

Having fled captivity and persecution in Israel and the Middle East, the Jews were apprehensive and unsure in India. One settlement became oil pressers, because that was low caste work, in order to keep their women from being raped by Hindus, the fear of caste pollution dominating lust among the ancient Indians. Today there are two major, but fading, communities of Jews in India: in and around Bombay, and in Kerala, a southern state which is located on the Malabar coast. There are some smaller groups in other areas. The greatest number of Jews totaled about thirty thousand at the height of their prosperity; now there are less than half that number.

Though the Bombay community is the largest and perhaps the oldest, the one in Kerala is the most famous and colorful, primarily because it has white Jews and black Jews. The white Jews are believed to have arrived at Cranganore early in the first century. I have been given different dates for the establishment of the first colony in this area; no one really knows and the date is immaterial. However, it is one of the oldest continuous Jewish settlements in the world outside of Israel. In the early period the Jews held slaves, a group of Dravidian Indians, the earliest inhabitants of the sub-continent. The Dravidians are dark-skinned, some so dark that they are blue-black. A few were converted, and lived as attached but subordinate members of the Malabar Jewish community. In the beginning they were not allowed to worship with white Jews. Tolerance came slowly and today, while they are permitted to pray in the synagogue, they may not read certain Scriptural passages.

In the sixteenth century the Jews at Cranganore were caught in a battle between two warring rajas, both brothers. The Jews were nearly exterminated by Muslim mercenaries and in 1567 they found refuge in the nearby city of Cochin (now the leading city of Kerala state). The Hindu raja at Cochin gave them a site adjoining his palace and they built a quarter called Jew Town, centered along a single street, with a beautiful little synagogue at the end. But there was to be no peace for the Jews. The Portuguese, who had been moving up and down the coast, establishing forts and trading posts, converting Indians to Christianity (with some force) and bringing groups of the St. Thomas Christians into the Roman Church, had already turned the Inquisition upon the Jews. For over a century, until 1663 when the Dutch drove out the Portuguese and established some freedom, the Jews suffered persecution. After the Dutch victory, the Jews were able to live in peace under various Indian rajas and then the British. But now the Jews of the Malabar coast have sadly declined. At the time of Indian independence in 1947 there were two thousand white Jews and nineteen hundred black Jews in Kerala. Today there are less than three hundred and fifty white Jews and less than two hundred and sixty black Jews. A small group of each still lives in Cochin, in Jew Town.

When I met a group of Jews in Bombay, it was like meeting a vestige of history, the survivors of a lost tribe (as they are believed to be by some romantics) who have endured the rigors of success and tragedy and wonder how they themselves escaped, and know that time is running out. One of them was a young man named Jacob Aptekar.

We are sitting in Jacob's aunt's apartment, which is a few blocks from the Gateway to India, a large triumphal arch standing on the edge of the harbor formed by Bombay and the mainland. Jacob's father is present along with some other men, and a friend of Jacob's named Isaac, who is trying to find a real Indian hippie for me. The hippie is said to hang around a nearby street corner and from time to time Isaac goes out to look for him. (I never found a real hippie; there was one boy in Calcutta who had dyed his hair orange-red and carried a guitar, but he was hours late for our appointment—I was on my way to another—and he never could be located again. He didn't seem at all authentic.)

One of Mr. Aptekar's friends gives me a pamphlet he has written on the Jews of India. It seemed rather forlorn when I read it later. The house is large, clean and cool, and Jacob's aunt, a thin aristocratic woman in a subdued yellow sari, brings soft drinks. Mr. Aptekar has a rarity with him, a bottle of imported scotch, which costs about sixteen American dollars when it is available.

The older men discuss the number of Jews left in India. No one is sure. Mr. Aptekar, who is a lawyer, thinks there may still be fifteen thousand, but another man says fourteen thousand—"I got it from a

Scottish newspaper, but it is last year's figure." A more pessimistic view is ten thousand, with eight or nine thousand in the Bombay area. Of the ten thousand, about one thousand are teenagers, a very small percentage, because in any population group today roughly twenty to thirty percent should be in that age bracket. Calcutta has five hundred Jews of all ages, Poona and Ahmadabad three hundred each. Cochin, the once-great center, and Delhi, about a hundred each.

Isaac rushes off on another search for the hippie, and Jacob and I go into the next room to talk. The furniture is large and heavy, very Victorian, with huge oak frames, glass cabinets with nineteenth century curios, and an old tape recorder. Everything must have been expensive once, and it is still the style that middle and upper class Indians admire today. Jacob and I sit down at a big oak table and Isaac comes in breathless and flops down in an easy chair in the corner.

> We Jews are withering away. We are going at the rate of seventy
> to eighty per week to Israel. At one time the exodus was one hun-
> dred and forty per week. We have to find a new life. Usually it is
> the young people who emigrate. In a few years I will go. Now I am
> learning colloquial Hebrew—I already know Talmudic Hebrew.
> We leave everything behind. Even if we sell all our possessions we
> are allowed to take only sixty-six rupees. [If larger amounts should
> be smuggled out they would be valueless: there is no foreign mar-
> ket for Indian rupees.]
> The Israeli Government pays for the plane ticket unless we
> have enough money to pay here. We go first by Air Iran to Tehran
> and then by El Al to Israel. The emigrant must work off payment.
> There's no prejudice against Jews in India . . . yet . . . No
> anti-Jewish feeling. But the political and economic climate is not
> congenial to Jewish life. Twenty centuries ago we were oil pressers
> and farmers. Later we became clerks and businessmen, lawyers,
> doctors, professional people, journalists. We were educated. Up to
> Independence we were quite happy in India. The British favored
> us because we were hard working, reliable and well educated. We
> had a kind of priority because the British took to the Jews and

liked them. There was a small exodus to Israel starting in 1944, and then after 1947 the exodus increased. The state is officially non-religious, but each group favors its own people, Hindus before all others, Marathis help Marathis, Sikhs help Sikhs, Bengalis help Bengalis, etc. Since we are small we are squeezed out, even though Jews have reached some of the highest levels in the Army and the professions and business. But in general, since there is no one to speak for us, a Jew has to go into business for himself. The Jews were always businessmen. The economic situation in India is declining but we have managed to survive.

Now they tell us, the people in the Government offices, the people at Air India, "Look, Israel is open to you, why not go?" We know we don't have a chance in these offices now; they favor their own people. Unfortunately the best men are not always at the top. The most we can hope for is a job as an ordinary clerk. It's very rare that a Jew gets a high post. People ask you when you are leaving India, even if you haven't said anything. They want your house.

The young people in our congregation have three classes a week of instruction in colloquial Hebrew. There are fifty in my class. We have some teachers who went from India to Israel and got established there and then came back to help us prepare for immigration. I also have two classes a week in religious instruction. We are studying the Torah at the synagogue—it's the rudimentary text with the dots. In the synagogue we use the book of prayer according to the custom of the Spanish and Portuguese Jews. My regular classes are at St. Mary's. The usual courses—Hindi, Marathi, English, elementary mathematics, physics and chemistry. Later I'll go to the University of Bombay to study chemical engineering. Then I'll emigrate to Israel. I should be about twenty-two.

I can't stay in India because I don't have a place. It's too expensive. Living conditions are quite low. If I can't go to Israel, I'll try England. Israel means hard labor, I understand that. But I'll have a future. There will be plenty of food. Everything is very cheap in Israel [this is an error; proportionately Israel is far more expensive than India]. Most of my friends have left. My current friends are members of other communities.

We are orthodox though we go to a liberal synagogue. I was bar mitzvahed at twelve. No candles. There are some Indian influences like certain sweets and foods. In the past we merged with the Hindus and picked up a lot of ceremonies and even superstitions, but once we were educated we gave them up. There has been a lot of intermarriage with the Hindus and even with the Muslims. This brought some leakage. It all depended who has the better hold, the boy or the girl. Some of the very strict prohibitions have gone—we don't have separate utensils for milk and meat, but we eat only orthodox-slaughtered meat. I had pork once, at the home of a Catholic friend.

Our name, Aptekar, comes from a village we once lived in. Most of our names are from the places of origin, like Navgawkar, Penkar, Cheulkar—the name of the town with "kar" added. We have the usual first names, Jacob, Isaac, David, Joseph and so on. One thing we didn't pick up from the Hindus is the caste system. We're just liberal and orthodox.

[The Question: who are you?] A boy, Jacob. Jacob. Jacob. Because I'm a boy and the boy's name is Jacob.

When we are finished talking, Isaac remarks: "In India there's no prejudice. There's no anti-Jewish feeling. I believe we can do anything we want if we want badly enough." Yet his parents have left and he plans on emigrating in three years when he is twenty.

We go into the big room. "There are two kinds of teenagers," says one of the men as we appear, "rich and poor. The rich are forward, up to mischief. They've got hobbies like music, photography, singing and games. The poor are not up to the mark. But once they go to Israel, they're OK, both types. Israel broadens them out, brings the poor up and takes the mischief out of the rich."

Mr. Aptekar remarks, "Nobody is thinking in terms of long-range planning. The time will come when the only Jews left will be parents and grandparents and great-grandparents. It's a transitional period.

Whether it will be tragic or happy, history will decide."

Jacob is apprehensive about going to Israel because of the language problem. He is slight, quiet and studious, and has a broader outlook than the other young people I have met. He is fifteen and has another seven years of study and work before he can leave. He is the only young person I met who was not condemnatory of foreign hippies. "Some people think hippies are millionaries, but they're harmless, they just want peace. They roam about looking at things." "Could you be a hippie?" "I could, I think. And I really don't believe they are wasting time, as other people say."

I ask Mr. Aptekar if he will be worried about Jacob's going to Israel if the war is still being fought. "No, not really. There's going to be a big outburst, then all will be settled."

On a Friday night I meet Jacob at Rodef Shalom synagogue. It is located near the botanical gardens and is unmarked. I have to go up and down a badly lighted side street before I find it, asking questions of small shopkeepers who know nothing of the synagogue. It is located on the top floor of a large old building. Beneath there seem to be apartments. The congregation numbers several hundred people, but only about two dozen are at the service. We talk before and afterwards, and I am given the names of relatives in Israel. Everyone seems subdued and low-keyed. This is a dying community, and in a year, two years, many of the young people will be gone. There is no rabbi. There had been one, a Rabbi Green from America, who came on a temporary basis and left in 1962. The services are read by a layman in Hebrew and in English by a woman.

A month later I visited Israel. From time to time one sees Jews from India: the older women still wear saris. They look out of place, but refreshingly familiar, among the energetic Israeli girls in shorts and military uniforms and Sten guns.

I lost my way one evening in Jerusalem. I heard a man speaking English so I asked him for directions. He was tall and brown-skinned. When he spoke again, I knew his origin. "You're an Indian," I said. "No, I *was* an Indian, now I am an Israeli."

Sultim Tenzin

IMMIGRANT FROM TIBET, Age 14

It is a truism that Southern India is much different from the North. In fact, India is somewhat like Europe in being, actually, a continent of separate states and nations, one as different from another as Sweden is from Greece or Poland or France. Southern India is lush and humid, more lush than the lush jungles of the North. The jungle becomes denser, more florid, more profuse as one goes south. This does not mean that the people have any more food: there are famines in the burgeoning floral jungles of the South just as there are in the arid plains of Haryana and Bihar in the North.

The quickest way south is by air. I am flying to Bangalore to meet a small group that is going further, by jeep, to the Cauvery River in southern Mysore to visit a refugee camp for Tibetans run under a tripartite agreement between the Indian government, the state of Mysore and the World Refugee Committee, which is an agency of the United Nations. About ten thousand Tibetans have been settled in Mysore in a very generous and courageous act on the part of the Indians, because their own people hardly have enough food or fertile land, and helping the Tibetans means antagonizing the Chinese, who have seized Tibet and either killed a large number of Tibetans or driven them into exile. In Bangalore I meet a retired Indian general who is the personification of the movie Englishman (he is to take over the direction of the camp), a true Colonel Blimp, with swagger stick, handlebar mustache, a pot-belly hanging over his belt, a floppy campaign hat, clipped English tones, and an Englishman's disdain for the foreigner (me) and the native, who is everywhere. The Indian army has been Anglicized to the bone. I suspect he would prefer to be sitting in his garden in his little house in Kent admiring the marigolds. Except that he is Indian. The General and I and a Captain drive for hours through the jungle, horn blowing constantly to warn off farmers, cattle, children and wedding parties (this is the auspicious season for weddings)—they are constantly moving from one village to another, the groom astride a white horse, probably for the first time in his life, on his way to meet his bride (whom he has not seen), proceeded and followed by musicians blowing on horns and beating drums with an eerie, tingling rhythm that always captures me. From time to time I want the Captain to stop so I can hear the music. But he is too contemptuous of natives, and we plunge on. Once we stop for tea in a village restaurant. I must explain that a restaurant in rural India is nothing more than a bamboo roof over a small stove, with a mud bench along one wall. The owner is solicitous of me and offers water. The Captain shakes his head. I know: germs. The water is not purified. The sun goes down in the usual explosion of pinks and reds amid the streaks of clouds. We plunge on with the headlights blazing and the horn making a single monotonous drone. Eventually we turn through a series of dirt roads, each getting worse than the preceding one, and at last we reach the Tibetan camp. It is very dark. There is a lot of confusion and milling around. The Captain suggests that in order to be comfortable the General and I stay at a *dak* bungalow, a kind of primitive motel designed for tourists, in a neighboring town. The darkness overwhelms us; there are no road lights. We run out of gas. It is pitch dark, and the only people around are farmers passing with their cows. A man from the camp who has accompanied us stumbles off in the blackness to find gas. Perhaps an hour goes by, as the General and the Captain and I stand in the blackness, with nothing to say to each other. The jeep is too hot to sit in, so we have to wait on the road. I have a slight fear of snakes—I have seen kraits a foot long which can kill in a matter of seconds, and cobras, who take a little longer— otherwise I tell myself it is an interesting experience, which it is. The moon appears and casts a wan light on the mysterious shapes that trudge by with their cattle. Finally the gas comes and we reach the *dak* bungalow. It is a masterpiece of tropical architecture, with a tile roof, a broad verandah, large high-ceilinged rooms and naked electric lights which have charmed insects beyond count, and a handful of servants who speak no English. The Captain gives a few orders and leaves. The servants bring tea and crackers. I notice that my bed, which is deeply concave, has a filthy mattress and lacks sheets. "Sheets," I say to a bearer. "Sheets. And a towel please." There are several bearers standing about in the usual crowd a foreigner attracts in India. "Yessahib," they all say, making it into a single word. Half an hour later there are still no sheets. I ask the General if he can ask the staff for sheets. He grumbles something which I take to be disapproval at my effeteness. I suspect he has sheets of his own in his duffle bag. Finally I take the table cloth off the table in my room—it looks like a sheet—it may have been—make the bed and drop off to sleep. The next morning I have a nice cold shower and let the water drip off me for a few minutes. The morning is cool and crisp but will rapidly become hot and sticky. The Captain returns to bring us to the camp. It is a long trip, I realize, up a macadam road, with the usual horn blowing scattering people and animals right and left, and then we take a dirt road for several miles, and then another which is pockmarked with holes and is being worked on by groups of elderly Tibetans in full winter clothing. The temperature in the sun might be about a hundred and ten degrees. In the camp we meet two young people who are helping care for the Tibetans, one of

them an English university student who has hitched all the way to India, and the other an Anglo-Indian girl named Valerie who has a lot of warm, funny stories about the Tibetans and obviously loves them. She remarks that the Tibetans suffer terribly from heat rash. "I asked some of the old ladies why they didn't wear lighter clothing," she reports. "But they said they prefer their winter clothing—'We Tibetans like to be warm.'" There is breakfast waiting for us: a real jolly English breakfast with tea, bacon and eggs, toast in racks which chill and harden it immediately, and butter and jam. I wonder if the General and the Captain will dress for dinner. That night I stay in the camp, sleeping on the ground in a palm-leaf shack, and feeling far more comfortable and at ease. The only problem in the camp is the latrine, home for a long poisonous snake which has frightened everyone.

There are, perhaps, ten thousand Tibetans in the Cauvery River projects, scattered about in camps. They are sincere, intelligent, hard-working people. A young American anthropologist who is working in one of the camps tells me that they are mechanical geniuses. "A Tibetan can study a piece of machinery, figure out how it runs, and build a new one." Some of them are now running farms, others are setting up small cottage industries, like rug-weaving. Everyone works. The Indian government gives each Tibetan of ten or older an acre of land. Thus a family of five will have a substantial homestead to begin on. The land is farmed intelligently and productively. The Tibetans know they cannot return to their homeland. Instead of brooding over the past and what might have been, as I have seen other refugee groups do, they are resolutely looking at the immediate present and the near future. Having been conditioned to the fierce cold and biting winds of the Tibetan plateau, which runs from twelve to eighteen thousand feet high, they suffer terribly in the lowlands of India. They have acquired a long list of tropical ailments which affect them more seriously than the neighboring villages of Indians. They suffer from eye diseases, summer colds, tuberculosis, heat rash, fungus and jungle sores, and malnutrition. Twice a day there is a clinic run by a young Tibetan woman named Ishi Sangmu, who has been trained as a nurse, and Valerie and Adrian the Englishman. In the past I have done a number of medical

Mother India's Children
and Mother India

Mother India's Children. After I had finished this book I realized that it is an oblique and very late answer to *Mother India,* written nearly fifty years ago by another American, Katherine Mayo. I had not deliberately written an answer. *Mother India* still bothers Indians, though few have read it. Something in the racial subconscious, perhaps. Miss Mayo objected to those aspects of India which any right-minded person would enjoy objecting to: caste, child marriage, arranged marriage, religious superstition, poverty, corruption and whatever else in other people sets our teeth on edge. She had a blind spot for England's exploitation of India. Miss Mayo had a lot of correct facts but put them together incorrectly and made a botch of analyzing them. Indians were furious (Gandhi's review of it was called "The Sewer Inspector's Report") and wrote many replies. One of them did the same kind of job on America that Miss Mayo did on India, with ample citations and photographs of lynchings, segregation, crime, poverty, corruption and child marriages (yes, America had them in the 1920's and still does, considering the very large number of teenage girls of all races and social classes, including the wealthy, who have babies without marriage. One sixth of all first children being conceived out of wedlock or before marriage according to one study I recall. India controls and legitimizes the natural instincts and is condemned).

Perhaps I am trying to deflect the inevitable horror and criticism of an India which ties young people into caste and arranged marriages and does not easily permit them to escape. I am not defending or attacking these institutions. They exist, and are facts of life. We do not understand them any more than Indians understand the tremendous freedom and responsibility our young people enjoy. Society is cemented together with a different glue in India, and the entire life cycle goes quicker than ours. The parents of most of the teenagers in this book had not been born when Katherine Mayo wrote *Mother India*. Many Indians, including these teenagers, may be dead at thirty, having just about had time to see their grandchildren. India will develop and evolve (or revolt) in her own way. We cannot force changes upon her people according to our will, mores, morals, laws, customs and history, as we have been attempting to do in other countries. Give help, yes, but not impose forcible change either through propaganda or active intervention. This is why I have tried to refrain from judgments: one must hope to See with the Third Eye and Listen with the Inner Ear and be paced by a Different Clock, and hope to be able to report what it is like growing up in India, as much as any foreigner can understand any other culture or civilization, or any person can understand another, even his own father, mother, brothers, sisters, or wife. Or children.

73-2438

915.4
R36

Rice, Edward.
Mother India's children.

Mount Mary College
Library
Milwaukee, Wisconsin 53222